D0122883

# As a Lady
# Would Say

# OTHER GENTLEMANNERS™ BOOKS

# As a Lady Would Say

## Responses to Life's Important (and Sometimes Awkward) Situations

### Sheryl Shade

## Thomas Nelson
*Since 1798*

NASHVILLE   DALLAS   MEXICO CITY   RIO DE JANEIRO   BEIJING

*To*

# CARRIE AND SHADE,

*two pure hearts that are at the core of my every thought. Thank*

*you for the love, joy, and goodness that you seek every day.*

Copyright © 2004 by Sheryl Shade, John Bridges, and Bryan Curtis.

Published in Nashville, Tennessee, by Thomas Nelson. Thomas Nelson is a trademark of Thomas Nelson, Inc.

**Library of Congress Cataloging-in-Publication Data**

Shade, Sheryl, 1958–
    As a lady would say : responses to life's important (and sometimes awkward) situations / Sheryl Shade.
        p. cm.
    Includes bibliographical references and index.
    ISBN 10: 1-4016-0150-2 (hardcover)
    ISBN 13: 978-1-4016-0150-8 (hardcover)
    ISBN 1-4016-0196-0 (leather)
    1. Etiquette for women. I. Title.
BJ1876.S53 2004
395.1'44—dc22                                    2004006466

Printed in the United States of America

08 09 10  WOR  7 6 5 4

# CONTENTS

# INTRODUCTION

A lady never intends to say the wrong thing. In a perfect world, she would always have her wits about her, impressing business clients and coworkers with her ability to think on her feet, always saying the compassionate thing in a moment of sorrow, never forgetting a name at a cocktail party. But the world is not perfect, and even the most thoughtful lady stumbles.

At times she may be able to laugh off her mistakes, but at other times she may find herself more than a little embarrassed by her own awkwardness. Even worse, she may fear that, without intending to do so, she has said something hurtful. A lady knows how to apologize, of course, but she hopes to have to use that skill as little as possible.

Thus, she tries to think ahead, and this book exists in order to help her prepare for life's most challenging moments. Some of these moments are predictable: At some point in her life, every lady will be called upon to express her sympathy to a grieving friend. At other times, however, she will be caught off guard by another person's inconsiderate remark or by the rudeness of a server in a restaurant.

Oftentimes a lady is put to the test when she least expects it. A longtime acquaintance strides up, extends his hand, and the lady's mind goes blank. A coworker has just had a miscarriage, and the lady wants to say something, but she does not know precisely the right thing to say. These awkward moments, and others like them, come to a lady far too regularly over the course of her life. In such situations a lady has no desire to laugh at herself, or at the behavior of others. Instead, she attempts to cope with such awkward moments by thinking ahead.

Rushing down the sidewalk, with six different things on her mind, a lady does not expect to run into her former boss. Neither does she expect him to be wearing an unflattering new toupee. But it happens, and her reaction to that person, at that moment, may say a great deal about her ability to deal with any of life's challenges. By saying the wrong thing, she may hurt a respected friend's feelings, changing forever the way he perceives her. By saying the right thing, however, she may shore up the self-confidence of a fellow human who may not be feeling entirely comfortable in his own skin.

A lady knows which fork to use, what to wear to a wedding at 7 P.M., and how to write a thoughtful, timely thank-you note. But being a lady goes deeper than following the rules. It requires preparation so that, whenever possible, a lady can do her part to make the world a much nicer place in which to live. Because she knows that a thoughtless comment can forever diminish another person's opinion of her, a lady thinks before she speaks, anytime, anywhere.

After all, a lady knows that in any awkward situation, the best course of action is to say as little as possible and to choose those few words with the utmost care. A lady knows that when she expresses her sympathy, she is not expected to heal the pain of parents who have lost a child in a tragic automobile accident. At the same time, she knows that even in lighter moments she is not perfect. If she forgets a name, she admits the gaffe and begs forgiveness. A lady knows, too, however, that she must stand up for herself and for her own beliefs and opinions. If a friend asks her to lie, she declines to participate in the deception. If she is treated rudely in a restaurant, she knows how to lodge her complaint—and how to determine with whom it should be lodged. If she has strong feelings about politics or religion, she knows when and where those opinions should be voiced. At the same time, she knows that being a lady does not require that she accept condescending or abusive treatment, in any situation.

In matters of love and friendship, a lady does her best to say the right thing. But she also knows that sometimes, when words seem to have lost all usefulness, her silence can be the most eloquent language of all. Knowing what to say, and more important, what not to say, in life's challenging situations is a priceless skill. No matter how awkward the predicament, a lady's goal is always to make others feel better about themselves, and she does so by attempting always to put herself in the other person's place.

A lady hopes that life will run smoothly—not just for herself, but also for the people she encounters in the normal course of her day. She intends to be part of the solution to life's problems—especially the ones over which she has some small amount of control. That, she knows, is what being a lady is all about.

# 61 THINGS EVERY WELL-SPOKEN LADY KNOWS

A lady knows how to begin
a conversation.

————

Although a lady would never
provoke an unpleasant confrontation,
she knows how to deal with one.

————

A lady always thinks before she speaks.

————

Although a lady does not fret
over the past, she also thinks *after*
she speaks, assessing the correctness
of her behavior.

————

If a lady realizes, in retrospect,
that she is guilty of an unintentionally
rude or thoughtless remark, she
attempts to set the matter straight,
at her earliest opportunity.

————

If a lady is subjected to a rude
remark or rude behavior, she does
not offer rudeness in return.

———

A lady allows others to finish their
sentences. Even in her most brilliant
moments, she does not interrupt others,
no matter how dull their opinions
might be—or how many times she
may have heard their stories before.

———

A lady does not talk with her
mouth full—even over the phone.

———

A lady is slow to judge the actions
of others, in either their public or
their private affairs.

———

Although a lady knows how to assert
herself, she also knows when to keep
her opinions to herself.

———

A lady does not take part in major arguments over minor issues.

———

When a lady learns that two friends are to be married, she tells the groom-to-be, "Congratulations," and offers her "Best wishes" to the soon-to-be bride.

———

A lady makes a conscious effort to use correct grammar, but she resists all temptation to sound stuffy and overly grand.

———

Faced with the option of using an unusual word or a word likely to be more familiar, she chooses the word that her hearers are more likely to understand.

———

Unless she is teaching an English class, a lady does not correct another person's grammar.

———

A lady does not use foreign phrases, unless she is absolutely sure of their meaning—and their pronunciation.

————

A lady does not pretend to speak languages that she has not made her own.

————

A lady is careful of what she says in the presence of people speaking foreign languages. They may understand what she is saying even though she might not understand *them*.

————

Even when speaking her own language, a lady does not use words that she can define only by looking them up in a dictionary.

————

Even in the most heated discussion, a lady avoids raising her voice. She does not shout others down.

————

A lady never asks another woman
if she is pregnant.

———

A lady never asks another woman
whether she is *planning* to get pregnant.

———

When a lady inconveniences another
person by asking him or her to shift
position so that she can move through a
crowded room, she says, "Excuse me."
She does not say, "I'm sorry," since there
is no reason for her to apologize.

———

A lady never says, "I'm sorry," unless she
has given offense.

———

A lady never begins a statement with
"I don't mean to embarrass you but . . ."

———

A lady asks no one—male or female—
to divulge his or her age.

———

When a lady initiates a telephone conversation, she knows it is her responsibility to end that conversation.

———

Unless it is an emergency, a lady does not leave overlong messages on someone's answering machine.

———

A lady does not use her cell phone when she is at a table with others.

———

Once a lady discovers that she must decline an invitation that she has already accepted, she promptly alerts her host or hostess. She gives a frank explanation of the reasons for her change of plan and offers a sincere apology.

———

When it comes to accepting social invitations, a lady never waits for something better to come along.

———

A lady does not engage in arguments,
of any sort, at the dinner table.

———

When a lady is confronted by
arguments that she considers foolish,
she does not attempt to refute them
with reason. Instead, she keeps silent,
knowing that logic is useless in the
war against irrationality.

———

A lady never claims to have seen a
movie she has not seen or to have read
a book about which she has only read
reviews. She knows how to say, "I
haven't read (or seen) that yet, but
from what I hear, it sounds very
interesting. What do you think?"

———

In civil conversation, and when
attempting to meet new friends,
a lady asks, "What do you think?"
as often as possible.

———

A lady gives direct answers, especially to controversial questions. She knows, however, that being direct is not the same thing as being rude.

———

A lady does not brag, especially about her own accomplishments or the accomplishments of her children.

———

A lady knows that the best kind of small talk consists of asking questions, not volunteering information about herself.

———

A lady never says, "I told you so."

———

A lady knows how to make an apology—and how to accept one.

———

A lady knows how to extend a compliment—and how to receive one.

———

A lady avoids backhanded
compliments at all costs.

———

A lady knows how to make
an introduction.

———

When it comes time for a
handshake, a lady extends her
hand, and is ready to do so.

———

For reasons of hygiene and simple
good breeding, a lady makes an effort
to keep her hands, especially her
fingernails, clean at all times. She
never knows when she will be
introduced to a new acquaintance,
and she never wants to feel reluctant
to extend her hand in greeting.

———

A lady always carries a clean
handkerchief and is ready to offer it in
times of great grief—or great joy.

———

A lady always attempts to make sure her breath is fresh, especially if she expects to be in close conversation with others. If necessary, she carries—and uses—breath mints.

———

A lady does not spread rumors. She is even careful about where she spreads sensitive facts.

———

When she is invited to participate in some pleasant experience—whether it is a dinner party or a major-league baseball game—a lady does not dally before saying yes or no.

———

A lady feels perfectly comfortable using the word *no*.

———

A lady understands the meaning of the word *no*, and she expects others to understand its meaning, too.

———

Whenever a lady requests any service or favor, she remembers to say, "Please." She is quick to say, "Thank you," whenever a service or favor has been offered to her.

———

A lady knows that listening is a skill that improves when it is regularly practiced.

———

When a lady feels that she has been subjected to an insult, she immediately knows the right response: She responds by saying nothing at all.

———

A lady has definite beliefs, but she thinks before voicing her opinions. She recognizes that other people's beliefs are valid. She argues only over an issue that could save a life.

———

In making after-work conversation, a lady is wise to leave her work at the office.

———

A lady knows how to listen.

———

A lady does not openly attempt to correct the behavior of her friends. Instead she teaches by example.

———

A lady takes no part in petty arguments over important topics. Instead, she takes action to bring about change.

———

A lady does not make promises she cannot keep. She does not make commitments she cannot fulfill.

———

A lady knows how to end a conversation.

———

# AROUND TOWN

## When a lady encounters an acquaintance who greets her with "Hi. How are you?" . . .

*She does not say:*

> "Actually, I'm having a lousy day. I'm retaining water, and I had to take the dog to the vet. What's worse, both my kids have the flu, and I think I'm coming down with it, too."

> "Just great. The promotion came through, and Ms. Bibs just had kittens. Want to see the pictures?"

> "You don't want to know—trust me."

*But she does say:*

> "Fine. How about you?"

In casual discourse, there are few questions that do not require an answer. This is one of them. Even on her worst days, a lady does not stop traffic on the sidewalk so that she can share her woes with an acquaintance who intended merely to say something a little more expansive than a simple "Hello."

### When a lady runs into a friend who has obviously had cosmetic surgery . . .

*She does not say:*

"Who did your work? I bet it cost a bundle."

"I guess I'm just not that kind of woman. Personally, I plan to grow old gracefully."

"When are you going to have the rest of it done?"

"It's none of my business, but I thought you looked better before."

"If I were you, I wouldn't have gone that big."

*But she does say:*

"Hello, Catherine (or Calvin), you're looking great!"

Whether she approves or disapproves of cosmetic surgery, a lady may encounter a moment of social awkwardness. Her friend has gone under the knife for the purpose of improving his or her appearance. Yet if the surgery has been successful, its results should be so natural-looking that they are not worth mentioning. A lady is better off mentioning a general improvement in her friend's appearance, avoiding the specifics at all costs.

## When a lady encounters someone who mistakes her baby girl for a baby boy . . .

*She does not say:*
"Are you blind? She's wearing pink."

"What can I say? She's bald like her daddy."

"I hope *she* doesn't get scarred from idiot remarks like that."

*But she does say:*
"Thank you; she is quite a little lady."

Since she no doubt has the most beautiful, dazzling baby on the planet, a lady realizes that people are going to be flustered by her child's beauty and there will be those who will rush to make a compliment, before they think about what they're saying. A lady accepts the compliment and in her own way lets the other person know that in fact the baby is her little girl. But she does so in a way that doesn't make the well-meaning party feel bad about an innocent mistake. If a lady has a tendency to be bothered by innocent mistakes such as this, she puts a massive bow in her daughter's hair, or dresses her in a romper set embroidered with "Little Princess."

## WHEN A LADY ENCOUNTERS A FRIEND WHO HAS OBVIOUSLY PUT ON WEIGHT . . .

*She does not say:*

"You still have such a pretty face, no matter how much weight you gain."

"You should look into that new surgery everyone is talking about."

"I know this great diet—if you want it."

"Why don't you meet me tomorrow morning at the gym?"

*But she does say:*

"Susie, it's great to see you."

A lady knows that another person's weight gain, or loss, is absolutely none of her business. She also knows that her wisest course is to shore up a friend's self-esteem, rather than destroy the friend's self-image. Weight gain may be the result of an incapacitating illness, stress, or some other emotional problem. When the friend eventually asks the lady's advice, the lady may offer it freely, always remembering the other person's feelings. Until then, however, she keeps her opinions to herself.

## WHEN A LADY ENCOUNTERS A FRIEND WHO HAS RECENTLY BEEN DIAGNOSED WITH A SERIOUS, PERHAPS INCURABLE, ILLNESS . . .

*She does not say:*
> "Have you told your children? I just don't know how they will get along without you."
>
> "Did they tell you how much time you've got?"
>
> "Do you have a will?"
>
> "You're looking really good, all things considered."

*But she does say:*
> "Hello, Jessica, how are you doing?"

When a lady asks this question, she is not asking for a prognosis, and she allows her friend to answer it in any way he or she prefers. If the friend is able to attend a party, clearly he or she would rather not discuss doctors and hospitals. The lady follows the friend's lead in the conversation and feels free to share the news of her own life, since that is very likely what her friend would rather hear. At the end of their encounter, the lady might, however, want to add, "Let's keep in touch. I want to hear how things are going."

When a pregnant lady encounters
someone who comments on how
much weight she has gained . . .

*She does not say:*
  "What's *your* excuse?"

  "How much did you gain when *you* were
  pregnant?"

  "Well, I think it's healthier to eat when you are
  pregnant than to try to fool people the way some
  women do."

*But she does say:*
  "My doctor says that my baby and I are healthy,
  and that's a good beginning."

A pregnant lady does not depend on
anyone other than her doctor to monitor her
weight. A lady knows that every woman's
pregnancy is different, and she keeps that in
mind, as she will no doubt be subjected to
countless critiques about her growing, and
hopefully glowing, body.

WHEN A LADY, AT A PARTY, RUNS INTO A
FRIEND WHO HAS OBVIOUSLY HAD AN
INJURY—PARTICULARLY AN INJURY
THAT HAS LEFT SCARS . . .

*She does not say:*
  "Did that hurt?"

  "Isn't there any makeup you can buy that can
  cover that up?"

  "Are you always going to have that?"

  "Has Michael been beating you again?"

*But she does say:*
  Nothing, unless a comment is absolutely
  unavoidable.

If a friend is on crutches or if his face is
swathed in bandages, a lady would be less than
human if she did not ask, "Gerry, what's
happened?" Still, she is discreet enough to allow
her friend to divulge as little, or as much,
information as he chooses. If it appears that the
injury has left her friend disfigured, a lady does
not comment on that fact, since it will probably
be part of her friend's life from then on. At any
rate, a lady never makes light of another
person's distress or discomfort.

## WHEN A LADY RUNS INTO A FRIEND WHO HAS BEEN FIRED FROM HIS JOB . . .

*She does not say:*

"So I hear you are going to be a stay-at-home dad now."

"How does it feel to have a woman supporting you now?"

"What kind of severance package did you get?"

"I wish I could get fired. I'd love to live on unemployment for a while."

*But she does say:*

"I hear you've left the bank. How are things going?"

A lady allows her friend to give the details of "leaving" his job. If the friend divulges the facts of his termination, a lady may respond by saying, "That sounds really, really tough," not encouraging him to rehash the painful saga. If the friend chooses, however, to discuss his job search, a lady is unfailingly encouraging, saying, "You're a bright guy, Alan. Once you're over this hurdle, the right door is going to open." She does not, however, overburden her friend with advice about what *she* would do. No two people's careers ever follow precisely the same track.

# WHEN A LADY'S GENTLEMAN COMPANION GETS LOST AND WILL NOT STOP AND ASK FOR DIRECTIONS . . .

*She does not say:*

"Why are you guys all such babies when you get lost?"

"If only you had stopped for directions earlier, we wouldn't be wandering around like this."

"If you're afraid to admit you're lost, I'll go in and ask."

*But she does say:*

"Perhaps I should call our host and let him know that we will be arriving a bit late."

A lady does not go out of her way to attack her male companion's ego. Instead, she calmly offers a simple solution. A lady knows that adding stress to a situation doesn't help—and that it increases her own stress level as well. If a lady realizes that a refusal to ask for directions is going to be an ongoing problem with an otherwise wonderful friend, she makes sure she knows the directions, writes them down, and allows her companion to see them, before he even puts the key in the ignition.

## When a lady encounters a friend who has obviously lost a great deal of weight . . .

*She does not say:*
"Have you been sick?"

"Are you sure it's healthy that you lost this much weight so quickly?"

"Well, you certainly needed to drop a few pounds. How do you plan to keep it off?"

"How much more do you want to lose?"

*But she does say:*
"You look fabulous. Is that a new dress (or a new sports coat)?"

It is not necessary to make specific mention of a friend's weight loss. When a lady compliments a friend's appearance, the friend will get the message and may likely be relieved to think the compliment is the result of a whole new sense of well-being, not just the loss of some extra pounds. If a lady has any suspicion at all that a friend's weight loss is the result of illness, she does not mention that possibility in public—neither does she spread such rumors among her acquaintances.

WHEN A LADY WITNESSES A WOMAN, IN
THE LATE WEEKS OF HER PREGNANCY,
PARTICIPATING IN A STRENUOUS PHYSICAL
ACTIVITY THAT MIGHT HARM HER
UNBORN BABY . . .

*She does not say:*
   "My doctor would never allow a pregnant woman
   to do that."

   "Don't you have a husband who can do that?"

   "Don't you know that you could be harming your
   baby?"

*But she does say:*
   "That box looks heavy. Let me help."

Many times a pregnant woman is convinced
she can still perform all of the activities that
were part of her daily life (such as carrying
heavy groceries) before she became pregnant.
Rather than offering a lecture or inquiring about
why the baby's father isn't on hand, a lady does
what she can to make the expectant mother's
day a little easier.

## WHEN A LADY WITNESSES A PREGNANT WOMAN PARTICIPATING IN AN UNHEALTHFUL ACTIVITY THAT MIGHT HARM HER UNBORN BABY . . .

*She does not say:*

"I hope you know that every time you smoke a cigarette, your baby's smoking, too."

"Have you ever seen a picture of a baby with fetal alcohol syndrome?"

"They should make women pass a common-sense test before they can get pregnant."

*But she does say:*

Nothing, unless she is a close friend or relative of the pregnant woman.

Regardless of her passionate beliefs, a lady doesn't walk up to complete strangers and counsel them on their personal business. A lady can only hope that the pregnant woman has friends, sisters, or a mother who will intervene before serious damage is done to the baby.

# FRIENDS AND LOVERS

## When a Lady Is Introduced to a Friend's Newly Adopted Son or Daughter . . .

*She does not say:*

"Don't worry. He'll start looking like you after a while."

"Look out! You'll probably get pregnant right away."

"Are you going to tell her she's adopted?"

"Aren't you kind to give a poor orphan a home!"

*But she does say:*

"Congratulations. He's a very lucky boy, and you're a lucky mommy (or daddy), too."

The adoption of a child of any age is—or should be—an act of love and a cause for celebration. In such situations, an enlightened lady does not pass along old wives' tales. Instead, she readily joins in the rejoicing, presenting the child with a gift if she feels the urge to do so.

## WHEN A LADY WISHES TO ASK
## A MAN OUT ON A DATE . . .

*She does not say:*

"I have an opening in my schedule; would you like to do something?"

"I've had a friend cancel on me; are you available for dinner?"

"Unless you are one of these insecure wimps who doesn't like for a woman to ask a guy out, I'd like to have dinner with you sometime."

"This is really embarrassing, but I think you seem like a nice guy. So I was hoping you would go to my best friend's wedding with me. Now don't prove me wrong."

*But she does say:*

"Would you like to have dinner with me?"

If a lady wishes to ask a man out on a date, she may do so, with no apologies or awkward explanations. A lady must, however, be prepared to accept *no*, and to handle herself with class and dignity, just as she would expect a gentleman to behave, should she decline his invitation.

WHEN A LADY LEARNS THAT TWO OF HER
FRIENDS PLAN TO BE MARRIED—AND THE
LADY FEELS THAT THEY ARE IN FOR BIG
TROUBLE . . .

*She does not say:*

"I certainly hope you folks have a prenup."

"You could do so much better. Please don't marry that guy."

"Why don't you just try living together first?"

"Let me give you the name of my lawyer. You're probably going to need it."

*But she does say:*

"That's great news. Have you set the date?"

Even if she feels that a marriage is doomed from the start, a lady does not consider it her duty to predict its failure. The bride- and groom-to-be might share interests of which she is not aware; they might have redeeming traits that are not evident; or they might, very simply, be in love. Now is the time for the lady to keep her opinions to herself. If the marriage should fall apart, no one will want to hear her saying, "I knew it would never last."

WHEN A LADY'S DATE IS UNDERDRESSED IN
COMPARISON TO WHAT SHE HAS CHOSEN
TO WEAR FOR A SOCIAL OCCASION . . .

*She does not say:*
> "I wish you had been more specific about the
> dress code."

> "I thought you said we were going someplace nice."

> "I keep a tie here just for this reason. Let me go
> get it."

*But she does say:*
> "If you prefer, I can change before we go out."

While creating as little drama as possible, a
lady simply adjusts her outfit, so that she and
her companion will feel more comfortable
during the evening. To forestall such
embarrassing moments, however, a lady makes
sure to ask her companion, well ahead of time,
about the plans for their date.

WHEN A LADY RUNS INTO A FRIEND WHO
IS HAVING DINNER WITH SOMEONE OTHER
THAN HIS OR HER SPOUSE . . .

*She does not say:*
"So where's Molly? Home by herself again?"

"Let me guess: This is your niece. Right?"

"Don't worry. My lips are sealed."

*But she does say:*
"Hello, Scott (or Paige), how's your dinner?"

The time is long past when husbands and
wives could be seen in public—or in social
situations—only with their spouses. In fact, a
lady may assume that if her friend is being seen
in public with an acquaintance other than his or
her spouse, nothing illicit is afoot. She may feel
free to introduce herself to her friend's escort,
should her friend neglect that casual nicety.

## WHEN A LADY IS CRITICIZED FOR NOT TAKING HER HUSBAND'S NAME WHEN SHE GETS MARRIED . . .

*She does not say:*

   "I hate his family name."

   "I'm not going to be a slave to that antiquated tradition."

   "Would you want to go through life as
   _____ ?"

*But she does say:*

   "We both prefer it this way."

There are times when a lady feels no reason to explain her actions to anyone except to those who are most affected by her decision. If a lady has decided to keep her maiden name, her decision is relevant only to her husband and other members of her family.

## WHEN A LADY IS CRITICIZED FOR TAKING HER HUSBAND'S NAME WHEN SHE GETS MARRIED . . .

*She does not say:*
"Well, you know about my problems with my father. Now, finally, I'm cutting at least one tie with him."

"Maybe I'm just not a feminist who rejects old-fashioned values."

"If you'd gone through high school with everybody making fun of your name, you'd change it, too."

*But she does say:*
"We both prefer it this way."

Although a lady might be tempted to encourage the critical party to get a life or take up a hobby, she simply smiles and knows she has no obligation to explain her choices to anyone but those affected by her decision.

WHEN AN ACQUAINTANCE REVEALS TO A
LADY THAT SHE AND HER HUSBAND ARE
TAKING FERTILITY DRUGS . . .

*She does not say:*

"Couldn't you just adopt? Think of all the
unwanted children out there."

"That's an awful lot of money to spend just to
have a baby."

"Which of you has the problem?"

"Watch out. You could end up with a litter."

"If God had wanted you to have children . . ."

*But she does say:*

"Well, good luck, Lori. I'm looking forward to the
blessed event."

A lady never passes judgment on this sort of
highly personal decision. Nor does she try to
make light of the situation. It is clearly a
weighty decision that will have long-lasting
effects. She wishes everybody well and resists
all temptation in coming months to ask, "How's
the baby making going?"

W<small>HEN A FRIEND ANNOUNCES THAT HE OR</small>
S<small>HE IS GETTING A DIVORCE OR SEVERING A</small>
L<small>ONGTIME RELATIONSHIP</small> . . .

*She does not say:*
   "Who's having the affair?"

   "Who's getting the Lexus?"

   "I know somebody who's perfect for you."

   "I hope you take him to the cleaners."

*But she does say:*
   "I'm sorry to hear that. Are you doing okay?"

I n such situations, the lady's friend may feel
sorely abused, and the last thing he or she may
want is a dating service. A lady need not
attempt to fix the problem; she need only
demonstrate compassion and offer a listening
ear. If both parties in the breakup happen to be
her friends, and if there seems to be no reason
to lay blame at anyone's doorstep, she makes a
special effort to avoid taking sides.

## When an acquaintance reveals to a lady that she and her current love interest met via the Internet . . .

*She does not say:*

"Be careful. I've heard horror stories about Internet love affairs."

"Don't tell too many people about this. They'll think you are a loser."

"Did the two of you have cybersex?"

"Tell me you didn't send him your picture over the Internet."

*But she does say:*

"That's interesting. Are the two of you having fun?"

Meeting via the Internet has come to seem no more curious than meeting on a blind date or through a personal ad in the newspaper. A lady might not think this is the wisest way to seek companionship, but she knows not to waste her breath giving warnings in regard to affairs of the heart.

## When someone criticizes a lady's significant other . . .

*She does not say:*

"I agree. I find myself saying the same thing all the time."

"It's something he has been working to correct for some time."

"You're one to talk—your husband is not only a drunk and a slob, but he's sleeping with his secretary."

"At least I have somebody."

*But she does say:*

"Excuse me, but I prefer not to discuss this with you. Perhaps, if you have a problem with him (or her), you should discuss it with him (or her) privately."

A lady does not put herself in the position of defending her chosen love interest to others. If an acquaintance insists on pressing the issue, a lady makes no bones about her intention to change the subject. If that course of action fails, she does not hesitate to walk away from the discussion.

# A LADY ASKS A GENTLEMAN
# FOR A DATE

In days long past, strictest etiquette forbade any lady worth her white gloves from even considering taking the first step in setting up a date. Young women were forbidden even to call young men, the assumption being that it was the gentleman's job to take the lead in any matter that might have the remotest chance of leading to matrimony.

Today, with women taking a prominent role in business and politics, living independent lives, and earning incomes closer to those earned by men, any lady may find it appropriate to invite a gentleman, whose company she finds pleasant, for any activity the two of them might enjoy. The steps she follows are not strikingly different from those a gentleman would follow in asking a lady to spend time in his company. In this situation, in fact, a lady may find it particularly easy to put herself in the gentleman's place.

When inviting a gentleman for a first date, unless she is in need of an escort to a major social occasion, a lady will be wise to suggest a casual evening, perhaps involving dinner and a movie. The lady broaches the subject directly: "I think you seem like a fun guy, Seth. I've been wanting to see the new Tom Hanks movie. If you're available Friday night, maybe we could catch it, and have some supper afterward." (She does *not* say, "I know this may sound silly, but I think you're really handsome, and I've always had this huge crush on you. So I was thinking maybe the two of us should get to know each other. What do you think?")

Should the gentleman accept her invitation, she makes all arrangements for the evening. (Even today, the gentleman will most likely offer to pick up the lady at the start of the evening, and see her to her door at the end.) She offers to pick up the tab for all expenses, except perhaps for casual expenditures, such as a pre-movie drink or popcorn at the movie theater snack bar. If the gentleman insists on paying for movie tickets or dinner, a lady sticks by her guns, saying, "I invited you, Seth. Let's at least go Dutch." If the gentleman seems uncomfortable with even that situation, the lady declines to make a scene. Instead, she simply thanks him for his generosity.

When inviting a gentleman on a date, a lady remembers, however, that she puts herself at the risk of being turned down—just as the gentleman would do, should he be asking her out for dinner. In no case does the lady appear insulted by the gentleman's refusal of her offer. (After all, she does not know whether he is already dating another person or simply may have other plans.) She may say, "Maybe some other time," leaving the gentleman the opportunity to say, "Sure. That would be nice."

She definitely does not turn on her heels with a high-handed "Well, you don't know what you're missing" or "What's the matter? You think you're too good for me?"

# WINING AND DINING

## When a lady's date insists on eating from her plate at a fancy restaurant . . .

*She does not say:*

"Didn't your mother teach you any manners?"

"Eat your own food! I don't share."

"You are embarrassing me."

*But she does say:*

"If you'd like to sample my entrée, let's ask the waiter to bring another plate."

A lady realizes that although her dinner companion may not have the most finely honed table manners, she never seeks to embarrass him or to give him an on-the-spot course in etiquette. If a lady feels that a gentleman is out of his league at a nice restaurant, if she chooses to see him again, she suggests that they might be more comfortable at a more casual establishment.

WHEN A LADY IS PAYING FOR DINNER
AND HER GUEST SUGGESTS ORDERING
THE MOST EXPENSIVE BOTTLE OF WINE
ON THE MENU . . .

*She does not say*:

"Wait a minute! Have you forgotten who's paying for this?"

"I'm sorry, but my expense account won't cover that. You're not *that* big a client."

"Okay, but it means *you* can't have dessert."

*But she does say*:

"I was thinking about having one of the Californias. They're a little more within my price range."

In such situations, direct action can prevent a great deal of embarrassment—either later in the evening, or later in the month when the lady discovers that she cannot pay her credit card bill. It is important, however, that the lady initiate this dialogue by asking, "What were you thinking we might order?" at a moment when the server is not hovering at the table. If the server returns before the lady establishes the limits, she unapologetically asks for more time.

## When a lady and her guests experience poor service in a restaurant . . .

*She does not say:*

"Are you just dense? How many times do I have to ask you for a glass of water?"

"Can't you get anything right?"

"I guess you don't know who I am, do you?"

"You just made a big mistake—I am normally a big tipper."

*But she does say:*

"We seem to be having a problem here. Would you point out the manager for me, please?"

A lady does not get into arguments at the dinner table with anyone—least of all with a server who is supposed to be making sure she has a hassle-free evening. When it is clear that she is not getting the level of service that she expects, a lady goes to the manager or, at the very least, the host. If that person cannot solve the problem, or at least find another server, the lady has learned an important lesson and does not take her business to that restaurant again.

## When a Lady Has Offered to Pay for Dinner and Her Credit Card is Rejected . . .

*She does not say:*

"Your machine must be screwed up."

"Run it through again. I know I mailed the payment."

"The good news is that I have twenty credit cards. I'm sure at least one of them isn't over the limit."

*But she does say:*

"Excuse me a moment. I'll be right back."

If a lady is dining in even a moderately fine restaurant, the servers and the management will do everything possible to help avoid embarrassment in this situation. Ideally, they will find an excuse to call her away from the table before giving her the bad news. If there really is a problem with her account and there is no other way of settling the bill (perhaps by running to a nearby ATM or convincing the restaurant to accept a check), as a last resort the lady might have to beg assistance from her would-be guests. Even then, she does not blame others, and she never, ever creates a scene.

## WHEN A LADY DISCOVERS THAT HER DINNER PARTNER HAS SOMETHING STUCK BETWEEN HIS OR HER TEETH . . .

*She does not say:*

"Don't you need a toothpick?"

"That cheese sauce really sticks to the old caps, doesn't it?"

"Oh my God—you are so funny looking."

"You saving that little bit of spaghetti for a midnight snack?"

*But she does say:*

"You might want to use your napkin. You have a little bit of spinach stuck to one of your teeth."

A lady alerts her friend, even if that friend is her love interest, the minute she notices an offending leftover morsel. No one wants to discover that he or she has gone through two cups of after-dinner coffee and a cognac with a strand of spinach stuck between his or her incisors.

## WHEN A LADY LEARNS THAT A FRIEND IS BEGINNING A DIET . . .

*She does not say:*

"This isn't one of those crazy cabbage-and-watermelon things, is it?"

"You? You don't need to lose weight!"

"Are you on another diet? Why don't you just give up?"

"You know, I was just thinking you needed to drop a few pounds."

*But she does say:*

"Good luck. I really admire your willpower."

A lady realizes that self-image is an entirely personal matter. It is not her place to judge anyone's motivations in beginning a diet. Nor does she dismiss their efforts, no matter how many times they may have tried before. She also knows that a huge percentage of Americans are technically overweight. Because she is a lady, she provides support and encouragement in any friend's drive for self-improvement.

# When a Lady Is in the Company of a Friend or Acquaintance Whose Actions Are Proving Embarrassing . . .

*She does not say:*

"Adrian, I'd like to come back here again sometime. But I'm certainly not bringing you."

"I hope you know you're making a fool of yourself."

"Everybody, I hope you'll forgive Martina for the way she's acting."

"Martina? I don't know anybody named Martina."

*But she does say:*

Nothing—at least not in front of other people, and not unless the friend's behavior threatens to cause a disturbance.

When a friend is behaving rudely, a lady has a couple of options: She may take the friend aside and suggest that the friend temper his or her behavior. Or she may simply tough it out, knowing that she need never spend time with that person again. Under no circumstances does she apologize for another person's behavior; neither does she attempt to embarrass another person in front of others.

## When a lady's companion wishes to order for her and the lady doesn't want what's been suggested . . .

*She does not say:*

"Not unless you want me to vomit at the table."

"I'm a big girl now, thank you. I can do my own ordering."

"This is the twenty-first century. Or haven't you heard?"

*But she does say:*

"Thank you for that suggestion, but I would really prefer the sea bass tonight."

A lady realizes there are several legitimate reasons a dinner companion may try to order for her at a restaurant, such as a desire to impress her with his knowledge of gourmet dining and fine wines, or a wish to give the lady a sense of his budget. Other motives, such as a desire to control the evening, should send up warning signals for any intelligent woman. The bottom line is, if a lady's dinner companion pushes her to order a filet when she'd prefer chicken, she speaks up and, if necessary, places her own order, directly addressing the server.

## WHEN A WAITER TRIES TO PRESENT THE CHECK TO A GENTLEMAN, WHEN A LADY INTENDS TO PICK UP THE TAB . . .

*She does not say:*
    "You better hope I'm paying—I make twice what he does."

    "Pig—why did you assume that the man is paying?"

*But she does say:*
    "Thank you, I'll take the check."

Although this may be a businesswoman's biggest pet peeve, she knows that making a public scene at a restaurant, or anywhere for that matter, is never an option. In a dignified way, and without preaching, she simply clears up the server's mistake, picks up the bill, and says "Thank you." She does not hesitate to write a note to the owner of the restaurant reminding the management that in this day and age women can and do oftentimes foot the bill for a business lunch—or even for a social occasion. She makes it clear that the servers at any well-managed restaurant should no longer make uncalled-for assumptions as to who is hosting the meal.

WHEN A LADY IS AT A DINNER PARTY AND
ONE OF THE GENTLEMEN AT THE TABLE
EXHIBITS BETTER MANNERS THAN HER
OWN ESCORT . . .

*She does not say:*
   "Watch him—you might learn something."

   "I would do anything if this clod would pull the
   seat out for me."

   "Sheila's got you well trained."

*But she does say:*
   "Thank you" for any nicety the gentleman does
   for her.

While it is natural to want to acknowledge
any extraordinary kindness, a lady never
purposely embarrasses anyone else at the table
by demeaning that person's behavior or by
pointing out the superior behavior of another
guest. A lady knows that a well-behaved person
does not appreciate having attention called to
his good behavior, except in the most
understated manner possible. In fact, she may
pass along the compliment most discreetly via
the gentleman's own dinner companion.

# ON THE JOB

## WHEN A LADY NEEDS TO BREAK OFF A TELEPHONE CONVERSATION WITH A LONG-WINDED BUSINESS ASSOCIATE OR FRIEND . . .

*She does not say:*

"I need to run. I've got something more important to do."

"Is this going to take much longer, Laurie?"

"Can you hold a sec?" (and then cut off the caller).

*But she does say:*

"I wish I had time to continue our conversation, Tom, but I've got a meeting (or a lunch appointment or a deadline) in a half hour. Now, what was the point you wanted to make?"

A lady need not apologize for gracefully ending a phone conversation that has gone on too long. Unless her business is customer service, she is not required to have her day taken up by intrusive callers. She attempts to complete her telephone business as expeditiously as possible. At the same time, a lady remembers what it is like to be on the other end of the phone and ends a conversation with a direct explanation that it is time for the conversation to end.

## WHEN A LADY'S FRIEND OR COWORKER HAS CHRONIC BAD BREATH . . .

*She does not say:*

"What crawled into your mouth and died?"

"Don't you think it's time for you to see the dentist?"

"You don't kiss Harlan with your breath smelling like that, do you?"

*But she does say:*

"I have these new breath mints. Maybe you'd like to try one."

Halitosis can impede the social (and professional) life of an otherwise wonderful person. So a lady is actually doing a kindness by letting her friend know that the problem exists. (The friend, after all, seldom smells his own breath.) If the friend declines the lady's offer of a breath mint, the lady is perfectly right to insist, saying, "Actually, Sylvia, I think you need one." If the friend's problem persists, and if she has not taken the hint, the lady might wish to try the breath-mint exercise again.

WHEN A COWORKER TELLS A LADY THAT HE
OR SHE IS BEING TREATED FOR DEPRESSION
OR SOME OTHER MENTAL ILLNESS . . .

*She does not say:*
"Does the boss know about this?"

"Did they start you on pills yet?"

"You're not having to see a shrink, are you?"

"I understand. This place drives me crazy, too."

"Don't worry. I won't breathe a word."

*But she does say:*
"Thank you for telling me about this. If I can help
in any way, please let me know."

Mental illness is no longer considered a
reason for shame and need not be suffered in
silence. When a coworker tells a lady about his
condition, he might very well be taking a step
toward recovery. Unless her fellow employee
volunteers further details, a lady does not ask
for them. Although she does not treat the
coworker's revelation as if it were a dark secret,
she resists all temptation to spread the news
among others in the office.

## IF A LADY FEELS UNCOMFORTABLE WHEN SHE IS ASKED TO CONTRIBUTE TO A GIFT FOR A COWORKER . . .

*She does not say:*

"Why should I give her a baby present? What's she ever given me?"

"You other guys may be pushovers, but you can count me out."

"What are you going to get? Let me see it first. If it looks like something I would buy, I'll give you five dollars."

"If I want to give somebody a present, I'll do it myself."

*But she does say:*

"Thanks for asking, but Marion and I hardly know each other at all."

A lady need not act like a curmudgeon when declining to participate in group gifts. As long as she makes it clear that she bears no ill will against the recipient of the proposed gift, she is perfectly justified in stating her position—and sticking to it. By refusing to chip in on the gift, however, she also forfeits her share of the cake and ice cream at the coffee-break baby shower.

## WHEN A LADY ARRIVES MORE THAN TEN MINUTES LATE FOR A MEETING . . .

*She does not say:*

"Sorry. I got hung up on some really important business."

"You folks are just going to have to forgive me. I'm always late—I'll be late for my own funeral."

"I can't believe you went ahead without me."

"Mind if we go back to the top of the agenda?"

*But she does say:*

Nothing if the meeting is already underway, keeping her apologies at a minimum until the group's business is finished.

When she is tardy, a lady does not expect the world to wait for her. If she makes a habit of being late for appointments, she understands that the business world will probably proceed without her. If she is a central participant in the meeting, she makes a special effort to be punctual. When she has an opportunity to apologize for her tardiness, she does so, without going into needless detail, but making sure to add, "I appreciate your going ahead without me."

## When a Lady Learns That a Friend Has Quit His or Her Job . . .

*She does not say:*

"Maybe you should have waited. It's always easier to find a new job while you're still working."

"You know, jobs like that one aren't a dime a dozen."

"Aren't you just terrified? I would be scared to death to not have a job."

"Are you going to sign up for unemployment?"

"I hope you didn't burn too many bridges."

*But she does say:*

"That had to be a tough decision, but I know you had to do what was right for you."

Not all career decisions are made on the basis of money. Although her friend may have had a great salary and wonderful benefits, the lady may not be aware of the stress taking its toll on her friend's sanity. While her friend is out of work, a lady may do what she can to encourage the friend to relax and chart a new course. It won't hurt, either, to take the friend out to lunch every now and then.

WHEN A FRIEND OR COWORKER ASKS A
LADY TO SUPPORT A POLITICAL CANDIDATE
WHOM THE LADY STRONGLY OPPOSES . . .

*She does not say:*
  "What do you think I am, a Nazi?"

  "Not only will I not vote for him—I am canceling
  your vote by supporting the opposition."

  "Do I look like a tree-hugger?"

  "I wouldn't vote for that fool if my life
  depended on it."

*But she does say:*
  "Thanks for asking, Renée, but your man (or
  woman) just isn't my cup of tea."

Unless a lady is ready to spend an hour in a
heated political debate, she will want to get out
of this situation as quickly as possible. She knows
that if her friend is involved enough to be
soliciting the lady's vote, there is little point in
the lady's attempting to explain her reasons for
supporting the opposition. She remembers that
ours is a free country and uses her time more
wisely, attempting to sway undecided voters.

## When a friend or a coworker asks a lady to tell a lie . . .

*She does not say:*

"You must have really messed up something bad."

"What's it worth to you?"

"You know lying is a sin, don't you?"

*But she does say:*

"No. I'm afraid I can't do that."

Nothing more needs to be said.

## WHEN A LADY IS TREATED IN A CONDESCENDING MANNER BY A MAN IN A BUSINESS SITUATION . . .

*She does not say:*

"Stop treating me like your daughter."

"I'm smarter than you, I have a better education than you, and I make more money than you. So just deal with it, jerk."

*But she does say:*

"I'm sure we both understand we have a job to do here. I would appreciate being shown the same respect I have shown you. Now let's get back to work."

A lady realizes that men who conduct themselves in an inconsiderate, condescending manner are unlikely to be successful doing business in the twenty-first century. When faced with such a social dinosaur, a lady does not stoop to his level. Instead, she sets a superior example by remaining businesslike and getting the job done. There is no reason, however, that a lady should be expected to forget such rude and potentially humiliating actions when she makes future business decisions.

## When a coworker takes credit for a lady's idea or accomplishment in front of other people . . .

*She does not say:*

"How did you come up with my idea?"

"You are a dirty liar."

"It must be sad to have to take credit for someone else's work."

*But she does say:*

"At the appropriate time, I would like to show everyone how we got to this point of the project."

A lady knows that, at certain points in her life, she will be faced with people who will go as far as to lie in order to take unjustified credit for an accomplishment. While she may be sorely tempted to call the liar on the carpet, in front of a crowd, a lady takes a deep breath and assesses the situation. In most cases, those who are most important to the job at hand probably already know the true story. But if a lady feels it is necessary, she finds an appropriate moment and shares the facts of the matter with the people who need to know them.

## When a lady notices someone eavesdropping on her conversation . . .

*She does not say:*

"Would you like to stand closer to me so you can hear the conversation better?"

"I'm sorry. Should you be included in this conversation?"

"Nosy, aren't you?"

*But she does say:*

"Let's continue this private conversation elsewhere."

While a lady never embarrasses another person by pointing out that person's poor manners, she is not required to tolerate rudeness. She knows that the best way to deal with an eavesdropping busybody is simply to move out of earshot or to postpone her private conversation until another time.

# WHEN TO USE FIRST NAMES

Although the world today is for the most part on a first-name basis, a lady knows it is always safe to address a new acquaintance as "Mr." or "Ms." She is especially careful to follow this rule of thumb if the new acquaintance is an older person or if she is dealing with her superior in a business environment. However, once Ms. Jones has told her, "Please call me Mary," a lady concedes to that wish. Otherwise, she runs the risk of making Ms. Jones/Mary feel ill at ease.

As a general rule, if a lady finds that a peer is referring to a person as "Mr. Brown" or "Ms. Smith," she may logically assume that that person wishes to be referred to as "Mr." or "Ms." She does not attempt to force business acquaintances to act as if they were her personal friends.

# AFFAIRS OF THE HEART

## WHEN A FRIEND OFFERS TO ARRANGE A BLIND DATE FOR A LADY . . .

*She does not say:*

"It all depends. What does he look like?"

"What's wrong with him?"

"If he's so wonderful, why aren't you dating him?"

"What makes you think I need help getting dates?"

"Thanks, but I've seen the kind of men you date."

*But she does say:*

If she is interested, "Can you tell me a little bit about him, maybe some of his interests?"

If she's not interested at all, "I'm sure he's a great person, but blind dates just aren't my thing."

A lady might enjoy the adventure of blind dating, or the accompanying anxiety may give her the hives. Either way, she attempts to be gracious to a friend who is, at least in the friend's opinion, trying to do her a favor. Whatever her opinion of blind dates in general, she can feel complimented that her friend thinks she's a nice person who deserves a little romance in her life.

WHEN A LADY IS ASKED TO ARRANGE A DATE
BETWEEN TWO FRIENDS, AND THE LADY IS
CONVINCED IT IS A ROTTEN IDEA . . .

*She does not say:*
   "Listen, he (or she) is out of your league."

   "You're too good for her (or him)."

   "I understand he (or she) has no money."

*But she does say:*
   "Sorry, friend, I don't play matchmaker."

If she is wise, in this situation, a lady sticks
by her guns and proceeds to change the
subject. In that way, she avoids making excuses
and forcing herself to find an explanation,
however feeble, that does not hurt her friend's
feelings. In such matters, however, a lady
attempts to be consistent, knowing that, even in
the best of circumstances, playing Cupid is a
dangerous business.

## When a Lady is Subjected to Unwanted Advances . . .

*She does not say:*
  "Not tonight . . . Not tomorrow . . . Not ever."

  "You sure do think a lot of yourself, don't you?"

  "You've got to be kidding."


*But she does say:*
  "You seem like a nice person, but no thank you."

The "you're a very nice person" line might sound trite, but it does soften the blow of the actual message. In this situation, the lady owes it to herself, and to the other person, to be absolutely frank. If the admirer will not take no for an answer, a lady has no recourse but to move, ask for the assistance of a manager, or leave the premises.

# WHEN A LADY'S DATE IS OBVIOUSLY BORED SILLY AT A MOVIE SHE CHOSE . . .

*She does not say:*
"Now you know how I felt at *Rambo 16.*"

"It says a lot about you that you can't appreciate a good film."

"You were snoring—I was so embarrassed."

*But she does say:*
"Thanks for going to the double feature of *Steel Magnolias* and *Beaches* with me. It takes quite a man to do that."

A lady feels no need to apologize if her companion doesn't enjoy a movie, or any event, as much as she does. In her life, she will no doubt be subjected to any number of sporting events, action flicks, and other two-hour entertainments that she does not enjoy as much as her date does. That said, when the next "women's" film is released, she remembers her companion's boredom and calls a girlfriend—even if the lady has just proven herself a good sport by sitting through an entire evening of fake wrestling.

# WHEN A LADY IS BORED BY AN ACTIVITY SUGGESTED BY HER DATE . . .

*She does not say:*

"You so owe me for doing this."

"I can't imagine how an educated person could sit through this mindless drivel."

"That was two hours of my life I will never get back."

*But she does say:*

"I'm glad I had the opportunity to spend some time with you."

A lady never consciously hurts another person's feelings, especially if that person's intentions were good. But if her tastes run more toward art films and wine tastings, she does not play the martyr by subjecting herself to a steady diet of disaster movies and auto shows. If a lady believes she might like a future with Mr. Boring Activity, she suggests activities she truly enjoys, offering the opportunity for both of them to find a compromise. (Perhaps he can spend his afternoon at the auto show, and she can meet him for drinks after her art-film matinee.) If the fellow can't take a hint—the lady takes a hike.

# AT A DINNER PARTY

WHEN A LADY HAS DIFFICULTY
UNDERSTANDING A PERSON WHO HAS A
FOREIGN ACCENT OR A SPEECH
IMPEDIMENT . . .

*She does not say:*

"Isn't there some kind of sign language you
people use?"

"Don't they speak English where you come from?"

"Wow! You must really have a hard time using the
telephone."

*But she does say:*

"I hope you'll pardon me as I want us to be able to
have this conversation, but I'm having a hard
time understanding you."

This sort of remark suggests that it is the
lady, not her new acquaintance, who has a
problem. It also provides her with the
opportunity, if there is a language barrier, to
bring an interpreter into the conversation. If a
speech impediment is involved, the lady may
suggest that she and her acquaintance resort to
pen and paper, hoping that, at future meetings,
the lady will become better attuned to her
friend's speech patterns.

## WHEN A LADY WANTS TO DETERMINE THE AGE OF A SOCIAL ACQUAINTANCE . . .

*She does not say:*
 "What year did you graduate from high school?"

 "Just how old are you?"

 "I bet you and I are about the same age, aren't we?"

 "How far away are you from retirement?"

 "If you were a tree, how many rings would you have?"

*But she does say:*
 Nothing.

There are hardly any social circumstances that demand that a lady know another person's age. Only when the conversation is related to shared experiences—and when knowing a person's age might provide an interesting point of reference—should the subject even be broached. Even then, a lady is content with a general age range. No further specifics are required.

WHEN A FRIEND ASKS A LADY IF SHE LIKES
THE FRIEND'S NEW OUTFIT AND THE LADY
FINDS IT UNATTRACTIVE . . .

*She does not say:*

"I'll say this much: Not everybody can wear
chartreuse."

"It'll probably look better after you've lost a little
weight."

"Shopping online again, huh?"

"You've got more guts than anyone I know."

*But she does say:*

"You always look great. But I have to say, that
cashmere sweater of yours is still my favorite."

A lady can avoid insulting her friend and, at
the same time, extend a compliment on the
friend's usual taste in clothes. What's more, by
mentioning a specific item from the friend's
wardrobe, the lady wins points for having paid
attention.

WHEN A LADY REALIZES THAT THE MAN
TO WHOM SHE IS SPEAKING IS WEARING A
NEW HAIRPIECE—OR HAS OBVIOUSLY JUST
HAD IMPLANT SURGERY . . .

*She does not say:*

"Hey, isn't there something different about you?"

"Can you wear that thing in the pool?"

"Guess you couldn't take Rogaine."

"You know, a lot of women really like balding men."

"Can I run my fingers through your hair?"

*But she does say:*

"It's good to see you, Chris. How are things at
the store?"

No matter how many people insist they
find balding men sexy, such compliments offer
little comfort to a man who is losing his hair.
To improve his self-image, he might go to great
lengths and expense. Such decisions may
appear superficial, but they sometimes stem
from deeply rooted insecurities. If a new toupee
or a hair-weave makes a man feel better, it has
accomplished its purpose. Unless she is asked
for her opinion in such situations, a lady keeps
her opinions to herself.

WHEN A LADY ENCOUNTERS AN
ACQUAINTANCE TO WHOM SHE HAS BEEN
INTRODUCED REPEATEDLY AND CANNOT,
FOR THE LIFE OF HER, REMEMBER THAT
PERSON'S NAME . . .

*She does not say:*

"Tell me again how to pronounce your last name."

"I'm having an Alzheimer's moment."

"I know we've met ten times, but it must not have
made an impression."

"I meet so many people; obviously, some names
are going to slip my mind."

*But she does say:*

"It's great seeing you, but you have the advantage
on me here. I'd appreciate it if you'd remind me
of your name again."

A lady knows that, in this situation, it is
best to bite the bullet and admit that she's
having a memory lapse. If she tries the "Tell me
how to pronounce your last name" ploy, the
name almost invariably will be "Smith."
Acquaintances might laugh off an occasional
gaffe, but if a lady habitually forgets a person's
name, she may need to try a little harder.

WHEN A LADY IS BEING ENTERTAINED
AT THE HOME OF A FRIEND, AND
SHE DISCOVERS THE FOOD IS
VIRTUALLY INEDIBLE . . .

*She does not say:*

"Does this shrimp taste kinda funny?"

"Just exactly what did you do to the rice?"

"Let me guess: This is the first time you've
made this."

*But she does say:*

Nothing, unless her host or hostess brings up
the subject.

If a lady is lucky in this situation, there will
be *something* edible on her plate, even if it is just
a carrot curl. That way, she can at least appear
to be having dinner, but in no case does she
force herself to consume food that she fears
might make her ill. If her host or hostess
notices that she is not eating, she admits,
unashamedly, that something is wrong. Most
likely, the host or hostess will realize the food is
bad and suggest that everybody head to the
kitchen for peanut butter sandwiches or skip
ahead to dessert.

When a lady discovers that a friend
has served her a dish that she
cannot eat because of dietary
concerns, medical reasons, or
religious convictions . . .

*She does not say:*

"I thought you knew I kept kosher."

"Don't you know what they do to baby calves to
make veal?"

"I don't eat carbs after seven in the evening."

*But she does say:*

"Sally, I'm afraid I'm allergic to shellfish. But I'd
love an extra serving of the salad, if it's available."

If her host or hostess has not alerted her
ahead of time to the evening's menu, a lady
with special dietary requests may be caught off
guard. In such situations, she has every right—
in fact, she has an obligation—to explain why
she is not touching the entrée. She is frank and
undramatic when explaining her dietary needs.
If her host or hostess provides an alternative
dish that is appropriate, she accepts it gratefully
and, if possible, makes a good show of enjoying
the dinner put before her.

## When a lady is embarrassed by her date's behavior at a party . . .

*She does not say:*

"I hope you have forgotten about what my date did at your party."

"You're not still upset about what my date did at your party, are you?"

"I apologize for Percy's throwing up in your ficus tree."

*But she does say:*

"I hope you know I've learned my lesson. I'm never bringing that goon to a nice evening again."

A lady never apologizes for the misbehavior of her date. But she does take responsibility for her part in whatever debacle occurs. (She admits her mistake in bringing Percy to the party, but she need not take responsibility for behavior that was beyond her control.) If any apologies are required, they should come from the goon himself. The lady, meanwhile, may wish to rethink being seen again in his company—at an event of any sort.

## WHEN A LADY RECEIVES AN INVITATION TO AN EVENT SHE DOES NOT WISH TO ATTEND . . .

*She does not say:*

"Before I commit, tell me whom else you've invited."

"I'll say yes, if it isn't another one of your drawn-out, formal affairs."

"I'm too old to go to your wild parties."

"Don't set a place for me. If I see you, I'll see you."

*But she does say:*

"I won't be able to attend. I have another commitment, but thanks for the invitation."

A lady need not go into detail when explaining her reasons for declining an invitation. She may find the company boring or she may know that the hosts invariably let political arguments take over the dinner conversation, but she does not mention such matters when responding to a request for the pleasure of her company. If she has no intention of participating in the occasion, she declines the invitation immediately. She need only remember that her response to the invitation must be kind-spirited and timely.

# HOW TO MAKE A TOAST

Over the course of her life, a lady will probably be invited to any number of wedding receptions, anniversary dinners, birthday parties, and other festive events. At some point, almost inevitably, she will be asked to make a toast, and if she is asked, she must not refuse. In this case, she does not attempt to give an after-dinner speech or perform a stand-up comedy routine.

Her tribute may be something as simple as, "Iris, I'm proud to call you my friend." She may choose to share some memory of her friendship with the honoree, or if she is confident of her skill as a humorist, she may toss off a lighthearted quip. In no case does she attempt to embarrass the guest of honor. Neither does she ramble on at length. A lady remembers that because toasts usually come late in the evening the wisest course is always to be succinct.

# AT A COCKTAIL PARTY

### WHEN A FRIEND OR ACQUAINTANCE COMPLIMENTS A LADY'S NEW ENSEMBLE . . .

*She does not say:*

"What? This old thing?"

"Well, you should like it, considering how much I paid for it."

"Harry will kill me if he ever finds out what I paid for it. This dress cost more than most of the people in this room make in a week."

"You don't think it makes me look fat?"

"Thanks a lot. I'll let you wear it some time."

*But she does say:*

"Thank you. I appreciate your telling me that."

Although a lady may think she is appearing modest, she is actually being rude when she declines to accept a compliment. Such responses suggest that she questions the taste of the person offering the compliment. If she chooses to do so, she may even reinforce her friend's opinion by saying, "Thank you. This is the first time I've worn it. It's a color I really like."

## IF A LADY NOTICES, MID-CONVERSATION, THAT A GENTLEMAN'S FLY IS OPEN . . .

*She does not say:*
   "So I see Mary Jane gave you red silk boxers for Valentine's Day."

   "Is it really going to embarrass you if I tell you your zipper is open?"

*But she does say:*
   "Jim, your fly is open."

There is no greater kindness a lady can pay a gentleman friend than to save him from potential awkwardness. If she and the gentleman are social acquaintance or coworkers, this is a problem that should be quickly taken care of, right on the spot. A lady does not attempt to get a laugh when alerting her friend that his pants are unzipped. If she and the gentleman are talking with a group of friends, she may simply place her hand on her friend's shoulder and draw him aside, tell him the news, and then let the evening proceed as if nothing has happened. If she and the gentleman are scarcely acquainted, however, she may ask another gentleman friend to pass the news along.

IF A LADY WISHES TO SMOKE AT
THE HOME OF A FRIEND BUT DOES
NOT FIND AN OBVIOUS PLACE TO
DISPOSE OF HER ASHES . . .

*She does not say:*

"Okay if I use this saucer for an ashtray?"

"Gee, I guess nobody much smokes around here."

"I'm just gonna have one. I'll put it out in the sink."

*But she does say:*

"I'd like to have a cigarette. Please excuse me
while I step outside."

In today's clean-air-conscious world, a lack of
ashtrays should be a signal to any observant
smoker. A lady makes the offer to enjoy her
smoke on a balcony, a porch, or a landing. If her
host or hostess insists that she remain inside, she
does not light up until a proper ashtray, or a
suitable substitute, has been provided.

WHEN A LADY, AT A COCKTAIL PARTY, ENCOUNTERS A FRIEND WHO HAS SUPPOSEDLY BEEN IN TREATMENT FOR ALCOHOL OR DRUG ADDICTION . . .

*She does not say:*

"Hey, I thought you were on the wagon."

"It's so sad that you are drinking again."

"I bet it's tough being around all this booze."

"Don't worry. I've got my eye on you. If you get into trouble, I'll drive you home."

*But she does say:*

Whatever she would normally say to a friend at a cocktail gathering.

A lady does not jump to conclusions or make hasty assumptions. Her friend's presence at a party may indicate that his or her recovery program is working well. The lady need not assume that the liquid in her friend's glass is anything other than sparkling water. Until she has reason to think otherwise, she silently congratulates her friend on his or her bravery in tackling one of society's toughest problems.

WHEN SOMEONE AT A PARTY PRESSURES A
LADY TO HAVE A COCKTAIL, ALTHOUGH
THE LADY DOES NOT DRINK ALCOHOL . . .

*She does not say:*

"Do you think I have to be drunk like you to have
a good time?"

"What's the matter? Afraid to drink alone?"

"You just want me to have a drink so you can have
your way with me."

"Okay. But just one."

*But she does say:*

"How about some soda? I don't drink alcohol."

A lady need not apologize for abstaining
from alcohol, no matter what her reason. She
does not pass judgment on her drinking friends,
nor does she allow them to pass judgment on
her. She feels no compulsion to explain why she
does not drink—whether for reasons of health,
religion, or addiction. She simply states what
she would like to drink and hopes that her host
will be able to provide her with a refreshing
nonalcoholic option.

WHEN A LADY, AT A PARTY, IS
INTRODUCED TO A WOMAN WHO IS
WEARING WHAT MIGHT VERY WELL BE A
MATERNITY DRESS . . .

*She does not say:*
   "I bet you'll be glad when that baby gets here."

   "When are you due?"

   "You must be miserable as hot as it is and as big as
   you are."

*But she does say:*
   "Hello. It's a pleasure to meet you."

Even if a woman does appear to be pregnant,
a lady can still enjoy making her acquaintance,
without mentioning that fact. If she is, in fact,
pregnant, she may be relieved to meet at least
one person who wants to talk about something
other than the impending arrival.

## WHEN A LADY HAS NEGLECTED TO RESPOND TO A PARTY INVITATION THAT WAS MARKED RSVP . . .

*She does not say:*

"Hope you don't mind my calling so late. It just slipped my mind."

"I knew it was a big party, so I just came anyway."

"I *can't* be the only one who didn't call."

"You mean there's not a place for me at the table?"

*But she does say:*

"I hope you'll forgive me for calling so late. I do hope you'll still have room for me at your party."

When a lady receives an invitation marked RSVP (an abbreviation for *répondez s'il vous plaît,* or "please reply"), she replies as soon as she possibly can, whether or not she plans to attend. Even if she postpones calling until the last minute, she still must swallow her pride and pick up the phone. If the host or hostess should happen to have filled her table without her, a lady has no right to be upset. Instead, she might say, "I understand. I hope you have a lovely evening. I'll try to have better manners next time."

WHEN A LADY IS AT A PARTY AND
SOMEONE SHOWS UP WEARING AN OUTFIT
SIMILAR OR IDENTICAL TO HER OWN . . .

*She does not say:*
"I'm embarrassed; I need to go home and change."

"Stan, let me have your sports coat."

"I am going to die. Now everybody will know I
shop where Nadine shops."

*But she does say:*
"I love your style. I guess we both have good taste."

A lady knows that if this is the worst thing
that ever happens to her, she has a sweet life.
What may seem like an embarrassing moment is
also an opportunity to display her self-
confidence and her self-effacing sense of humor.

WHEN A LADY NOTICES THAT ANOTHER
LADY AT A PARTY HAS STUFFED HER SKIRT
INTO HER PANTY HOSE . . .

*She does not say:*
"I am so embarrassed for you."

"Darling, you are mooning everyone at this shindig."

"All eyes are on you tonight and not for the
reason you are hoping."

"Trying to spice up the party?"

*But she does say:*
"Excuse me; let's step into the hall."

One lady does not hesitate to help another,
whether they are new acquaintances or longtime friends. She trusts that should she be
found in the same situation, another lady would
offer her the same kindness.

## WHEN A LADY NOTICES THAT ANOTHER LADY HAS A STREAMER OF TOILET PAPER STUCK TO ONE OF HER HEELS . . .

*She does not say:*
"Saving some to take home?"

"You are going to die when you know what is on your shoe, and that you have been walking around this party for an hour like that."

*But she does say:*
"Excuse me, but you have some toilet paper stuck to one of your heels."

When a lady is dragging a toilet-paper streamer across a crowded drawing room, the sooner it is brought to her attention, the better. There is hardly any way to bring the trailing tissue to a lady's attention without others noticing. However, at such a moment, the best another lady can do is to offer a shoulder to lean on and the commiserating comfort that "It happens to all of us."

# THE HOSTESS
# WITH THE MOST

## WHEN A LADY RECEIVES A GIFT THAT IS THE DUPLICATE OF SOMETHING SHE ALREADY OWNS . . .

*She does not say:*

"You know, when I bought my first one of these, I thought how much I'd really like to have two of them."

"I guess great minds think alike."

"You didn't happen to keep the receipt, did you?"

*But she does say:*

"What a great gift! I love it!"

In this situation, a lady's gratitude can be genuine and exuberant; she recognizes that her friend does indeed know the lady's taste. The friend knows it so well, in fact, that he or she has purchased just the sort of thing the lady would buy for herself. The best part is that even after the lady has exchanged the duplicate gift, she can continue to use the original, and her friend will be none the wiser.

WHEN A FRIEND PRESENTS A LADY WITH A
GIFT THAT IS OBVIOUSLY MUCH MORE
EXPENSIVE THAN THE GIFT THE LADY HAS
BOUGHT FOR HER FRIEND . . .

*She does not say:*

"Wow, you certainly made me look cheap."

"Of course, this is only part of your gift. The rest
of it hasn't come in yet."

"I really hate show-offs."

*But she does say:*

"Thank you. What a beautiful gift."

When a lady has received a particularly
generous gift, she may be as effusive as she likes in
expressing her gratitude, but she knows that her
friend would be made uncomfortable if the lady
were to apologize or appear embarrassed about
the less expensive gift she has presented. She
trusts that her friend appreciates her gift for the
sentiment it expresses—not for the size of its price
tag. Gift giving is not a competition sport. Because
gifts are a sign of generosity and appreciation,
whenever they are offered, everybody wins.

WHEN A LADY OPENS HER PRESENT AND
DISCOVERS THAT IT OBVIOUSLY COST
MUCH LESS THAN THE ONE SHE
PURCHASED FOR HER FRIEND . . .

*She does not say:*
   "Little things mean a lot."

   "Is this all?"

   "I'm always impressed with what you can do with
   five dollars."

*But she does say:*
   "Thank you. What a lovely gift."

A lady does not rate gifts by the size of
their price tags. She does not, in fact, rate them
on any basis. She knows that her friend may
have invested many hours in selecting even the
simplest gift. She would never belittle that
effort. To do so would imply that she selects
her friends on the basis of their annual incomes.

## WHEN A FRIEND LIGHTS UP A CIGARETTE IN A LADY'S SMOKE-FREE HOME . . .

*She does not say:*

"What are you trying to do . . . kill us all?"

"You can smoke up your own house if you want to, Jason, but get that stuff out of my house."

"Do you see any ashtrays around here, Barbara? Can't you take a hint?"

*But she does say:*

"Jason, you'll find an ashtray out on the balcony. I keep it there for my friends who smoke."

A lady has the right to live in a smoke-free environment, but she might want to entertain smokers in her home from time to time. Once they are her guests, she would never attempt to insult them. Thus, she plans ahead, thinking of her friends' convenience and—as much as possible, in inclement weather—their health.

WHEN A GUEST BREAKS A PIECE OF CHINA
(OR A VASE OR A GLASS) AT A PARTY WHERE
A LADY IS HOSTESS . . .

*She does not say:*

"Do you know what a plate like that *costs?*"

"That can't be replaced. It was a family heirloom."

"Luckily, you can buy me a replacement at Nordstrom's."

"The least you can do is start cleaning up the mess."

"Next time, I'm using Chinet."

*But she does say:*

"Are you all right, Marvin? I hope you didn't cut yourself."

When a lady entertains regularly, she quickly learns that broken china and glassware are a part of life. When a plate or a glass gets broken, she expresses concern for the welfare of her guest, not for the loss of the dinner plate or goblet. If the guest should offer to pay for the breakage, the lady refuses the offer. If her china is more important to her than her friends, she either leaves her china in the cabinet, or she dines alone.

## WHEN A LADY REALIZES THAT SHE HAS PREPARED A DINNER THAT IS, FOR WHATEVER REASON, INEDIBLE . . .

*She does not say:*

"I hope you don't mind if it's a little burned. You can scrape off the crusty bits."

"I'm sorry it tastes like this. You're lucky there's a McDonald's on the way home."

"Does it taste strange to you? It tastes perfectly fine to me."

*But she does say:*

"Who likes pepperoni?"

Even the most meticulous lady makes mistakes, and because she is a lady, she admits them readily. If she has burned the chicken or if the pork chops taste funny, she knows she does not have to cancel her party. Instead, she immediately orders take-out, for which she, of course, picks up the tab. That way, she will be remembered for her grace under fire, not for a night in the emergency room.

WHEN A LADY HAS PREPARED DINNER
AND LEARNS THAT A FRIEND—FOR
WHATEVER REASON—CANNOT EAT THE
FOOD SHE HAS COOKED . . .

*She does not say:*

"It won't make you really sick, will it?"

"Aren't you taking this no-carb thing a little far?"

"So what if you're a vegetarian? Fish isn't meat."

*But she does say:*

"I'm sorry, Barbara. I should have mentioned what
I was planning to serve. Can I give you a little
more salad?"

In today's society, no lady should be
surprised to discover that a friend—for
whatever reasons—may decline to eat certain
foods. When extending a dinner invitation, she
suggests the menu she has in mind, hoping that
her friend will let her know if it includes
something he or she cannot eat. If such is the
case, she reworks her menu or, at the very least,
she provides alternatives. If, however, she
discovers too late that her friend cannot eat the
lovingly prepared dinner, the lady does her best
to come up with a quick substitute.

## WHEN A LADY, AS HOSTESS OF A PARTY, REALIZES THAT ONE OF HER GUESTS HAS HAD TOO MUCH TO DRINK . . .

*She does not say:*
"Finish that drink while I make a pot of coffee."

"Don't leave until I can find somebody to follow you."

"Honey, if you don't realize how drunk you are, you've got a real problem."

*But she does say:*
"Carla, you've had plenty to drink, and I'm concerned about your safety. Just to be safe, give me your keys; we're going to get you a cab home."

A lady does not attempt to reason with a friend who has been overserved. Instead, the lady takes charge, accepts no arguments to the contrary, and makes sure her friend gets home safely. (Sending another partygoer to tail the drunk driver accomplishes absolutely nothing.) The friend might protest and even become confrontational. But in the morning, or at least by the next afternoon, he or she will be grateful. Better yet, the friend will still be alive.

WHEN A LADY HAS NO CHOICE BUT TO
TAKE AN IMPORTANT PHONE CALL WHILE
ENTERTAINING FRIENDS OR CONDUCTING A
BUSINESS MEETING . . .

*She does not say:*

"You folks don't mind if I take this call, do you?"

"Keep yourselves entertained. I'd better catch
this one."

"Don't listen to this. Just talk among yourselves."

"I know this is rude, but I'm gonna do it anyway."

*But she does say:*

"Excuse me, please. I need to take this call. I'll try
to make it quick."

On rare occasions there may be emergencies
or heat-of-the-moment business calls that
require a lady's immediate attention, but those
are the only times she is justified in abandoning
her friends or business associates in order to talk
on the phone. If a lady knows the interrupting
call is a possibility before the gathering gets
under way, she alerts her guests to that
possibility. In all cases, if she must take this sort
of call, she does so in another room. That way,
the gathering can continue in her absence.

WHEN A LADY IS HOSTING A SEATED
DINNER PARTY AND AN INVITED GUEST
CALLS TO ASK WHETHER HE OR SHE MAY
BRING AN ADDITIONAL FRIEND, FOR WHOM
THE LADY DOES NOT HAVE ROOM . . .

*She does not say:*
  "How dare you ask such a thing?"

  "Okay, but he's got to bring his own steak."

  "Bring him along, but it's going to make
  everybody very uncomfortable."

*But she does say:*
  "I'd love for you to bring Jim (or Jessica), but I'm
  afraid I've only got room at the table for eight.
  Maybe he can come along some other time."

When a friend calls with this kind of
request, he or she should expect to get a frank
response. A lady tries to plan her parties so that
everyone will have a good time. She knows
whether there is room at her table for an extra
plate. If an extra chair would cause everyone to
be knocking elbows, she does not attempt to
crowd in an extra body.

## WHEN A LADY FEELS IT IS TIME TO CHANGE THE TOPIC OF THE CONVERSATION AT A PARTY . . .

*She does not say:*

"Enough about that. Let's talk about Miranda's new nose job."

"I hate to interrupt you, Rosie, but before I forget it, I wanted to tell my new joke."

"Martha—you're about to piss everyone off again—so change the subject."

"Are you people as bored with this conversation as I am?"

*But she does say:*

"This might not be exactly on the subject, but your comment reminds me of something I read the other day in *Vanity Fair.*"

Because she is a skillful conversationalist, a lady is adept at guiding table talk. If a less creative guest continues to return to the exhausted topic, the lady may persevere, interjecting when possible, "Yes, but don't you think it's interesting that . . ." If a lady feels that the tenor of the conversation is growing tasteless or potentially incendiary, she has every right to say, "I think maybe we should talk about something else."

## WHEN A LADY HAS A PROBLEM WITH EMPLOYEES AT HER DINNER PARTY . . .

*She does not say:*
"Don't embarrass me in front of my guests."

"Please leave, so I don't start screaming."

"I should have listened to Amy when she told me you were a bartender who drinks more than the guests."

*But she does say:*
"Sharon (or Andrew), may I see you for a moment in the kitchen?"

Regardless of the seriousness of the problem, a lady does not embarrass her guests, the offending employees, and herself by confronting an unsatisfactory server or bartender in front of her guests. She simply handles the problem calmly and quickly so she can get back to her role as hostess. If the situation is so dire that she must dismiss the employee, mid-party, she does the best she can to make the evening a success, asking friends to pitch in by helping tend bar or by passing the hors d'oeuvres.

## WHEN A LADY NEEDS TO RECALL AN INVITATION BY TELEPHONE . . .

*She does not say:*

"Something came up and we need to cancel the event."

"We're going to have to cancel tonight's cookout. Tom just offered me Bette Midler tickets."

*But she does say:*

"Rhonda, I am so sorry, but I am not feeling well, and we are going to have to cancel the party tonight. Thank you in advance for understanding, and I will be in touch soon to reschedule."

While unfortunate, it is inevitable that a lady will occasionally have to cancel a party she has scheduled—due to a sudden illness or a family emergency. In such instances, she must contact her guests as soon as possible. Those messages should be given in person over the telephone, with a voice mail message as a last resort. Under no circumstances does a lady cancel an event she is hosting simply because a better offer comes up—even if it does involve Bette Midler.

# HOW TO MAKE AN
# INTRODUCTION

Even in our increasingly casual society, a
lady respects the time-honored traditions
surrounding social introductions.

• A younger person is always introduced to an
  older person. For example, when Larry
  Lyons, who is in his twenties, is introduced
  to Mr. Allgood, who is in his fifties, a lady
  says, "Mr. Allgood, I'd like you to meet Larry
  Lyons." Even if a younger woman is being
  introduced to an older man, a lady makes
  sure to say the older person's name first.

• When a lady introduces a man and a woman
  who are of essentially the same age, she
  introduces the man *to* the woman. Thus, if
  her friends Sally Baldwin and Larry Lyons do
  not know each other, a lady introduces them
  by saying, "Sally, this is my friend Larry
  Lyons." Then the lady turns to Larry and
  says, "Larry, this is Sally Baldwin."

• In all cases, a lady feels free to add some
  detail to stimulate conversation. She might
  say, for example, "Mr. Allgood, Larry is one

of my good friends from law school." Or "Sally, you must have heard me talk about Larry. We went to the Harry Connick Jr. concert last week."

- Unless she is being introduced to a dignitary, it is always a lady's responsibility to extend her hand for a handshake, no matter what the age of the gentleman to whom she is being introduced.

- When being introduced to a young boy, a lady makes the offer of a handshake. If the boy has not had practice in the art of handshaking, the lady simply gives him a pat on the shoulder and says, "It's awfully nice to meet you, Sam."

- A lady makes every effort to pronounce names clearly. If it is convenient, she repeats the names at some not-too-distant point in the conversation.

Even if she is uncertain of the protocol of the moment, however, a lady always does her best to make an introduction. Even if she makes a small mistake, she has not committed the more serious error of being rude.

# HOW TO START A
# CONVERSATION

At a party, a reception, or a business meeting, a lady feels free to strike up a conversation with any pleasant person she encounters. To prevent awkwardness, however, she begins with positive, noncontroversial subject matter. She might say, "This is a nice party, isn't it?" or "Charlie has certainly done a good job of bringing this meeting together, hasn't he?"

In every case, a lady begins by asking a question that does not bring the conversation around to herself. If the person standing next to her responds cordially, she continues with a few more questions until the conversation is under way. She might venture out by asking, for example, "Did you see the Westminster dog show last week?" But she knows that she is still testing the waters.

Never, or at least not until the conversation is well under way, does she venture into uncharted territory, such as the lukewarm food on the buffet or the recent downslide in the company stock. Invariably, after she has made this sort of comment, a lady discovers that she is speaking to the hostess's sister or the boss's son.

# HOW TO END A CONVERSATION

A lady recognizes that every conversation has its own natural rhythm. She is not being rude or inconsiderate when she attempts to bring any conversation—no matter how pleasant or important—to a timely close.

When talking on the telephone, a lady accepts the responsibility for ending any conversation she has begun. When the conversation is taking place in her office, it is a lady's responsibility to bring the meeting to a close. In every case, she states as directly as possible that it is time for the discussion to end; she does not allow the conversation to dawdle along uncomfortably. On the telephone, she might say something as simple as, "It's been very good talking to you, Joan. I hope we get to talk again soon." In person, she stands up, thanks her guest for meeting with her, and extends her hand for a handshake.

In a social setting such as cocktail party, a lady simply excuses herself by telling her conversation partner that she is going to mingle, or if the hour is late, head for home. She ends that conversation by saying that she enjoyed the other person's company and hopes they can talk again soon.

# PRIVATE LIVES

## WHEN A LADY'S EVENING IS INTERRUPTED BY A TELEMARKETER . . .

*She does not say:*

"How does it feel to spend your life irritating people?"

"Give me your home number. I want to call you tomorrow night when *you're* trying to have dinner."

"Is this the only job you could get?"

"You know you're breaking the law. I could have you arrested if I weren't so nice."

*But she does say:*

"No thanks. Don't call me again. Good night."

Telemarketers, for good or ill, are simply doing the job they were hired to do. A lady does not attempt to insult them. She remains polite and courteous, even with those who may be annoying. She is direct and makes it clear that she does not wish to be called again. Then she returns to her dinner and gets on with her life.

WHEN AN ACQUAINTANCE ASKS A LADY
HOW OLD SHE IS, AND SHE PREFERS NOT
TO DISCUSS HER AGE . . .

*She does not say:*

"How old do you think I am?"

"It's rude to ask a lady her age."

"How old do I look?"

"Why are you asking?"

*But she does say:*

"Sorry, but I don't give out that information."

Even if she offers this sort of response in a lighthearted manner, a lady will still let it be known that she wants to talk about something else. More often than not, when a friend asks a lady's age, the friend intends, eventually, to offer a compliment. Still, for whatever reasons, a lady has the right to keep any of her vital statistics to herself.

W<small>HEN A FRIEND DROPS BY UNANNOUNCED</small>
<small>AND A LADY IS NOT IN THE MOOD FOR—</small>
<small>OR PREPARED FOR—COMPANY . . .</small>

*She does not say:*

"I've got the flu. Go away; I don't want you to catch it."

"My house is a wreck. I wouldn't even let my mother in here today."

"Didn't your mother teach you any manners?"

*But she does say:*

"Thanks for dropping by, Mary Kay, but this is a bad time for me. Give me a call, and we'll get together sometime soon."

A lady feels no obligation to invite an unexpected guest into her home. Otherwise, she will be stuck with the dilemma of finding a gracious way to get him or her to leave. Instead, a lady recommends that the unwanted guest give her a call to set up their next meeting, suggesting that she would enjoy the friend's company, but not at that precise moment.

## WHEN AN ACQUAINTANCE ASKS A LADY TO REVEAL HER SALARY . . .

*She does not say:*
   "Not as much as I'm worth."

   "That's none of your business."

   "More than you, I'm sure of that."

   "What a tacky question!"

*But she does say:*
   "I prefer not to talk about salaries."

A lady makes it clear that she does not discuss *anyone's* personal income. She knows that her salary is part of a confidential agreement between her and her employer. If she is wise, she will keep it that way. Without fail, once she has revealed how much she makes, some will feel that she is being overcompensated, while others will pity her for being paid so little. A potential suitor may even confront a lady about her income because he is uncomfortable dating a woman who makes more money than he does—or he may actually be looking for a woman who can afford to take care of him. Either way, a lady is wise to keep information about her income to herself.

WHEN A LADY, ON AN AIRPLANE, TRAIN,
OR BUS IS SEATED NEXT TO A FELLOW
TRAVELER INTENT ON HAVING A
CONVERSATION . . .

*She does not say:*
   "That's a fascinating story. Maybe the guy in the
   aisle seat would like to hear it."

   "Sorry, I'm not feeling well. I've got the flu."

*But she does say:*
   "I wish I were able to talk with you, but I have to
   finish this paperwork (or read this article) before
   the end of the flight."

When travelers are seated beside one
another on an airplane, they are not required
to—or even expected to—establish a social
relationship. If a lady and a fellow traveler are
in the mood to talk, they may enjoy each
other's company. But a lady feels no obligation
to become best friends with her temporary
next-door neighbor. If the two of them do
strike up a conversation, however, they talk
quietly, so as not to disturb other passengers.

## WHEN SOMEONE QUESTIONS A LADY'S PATRIOTISM OR HER CANDIDATE OF CHOICE . . .

*She does not say:*

"I had no idea you were such a liberal."

"What proof do you have that *you're* such a great American?"

"You are really embarrassing yourself by this stance, Ann. Everybody is talking about it."

*But she does say:*

"I've always believed our nation's greatest strength is that it allows us to tolerate our differences. So let's just agree to disagree on this."

In today's ever-changing political climate, a lady will at one time or another probably come into contact with another person who feels so strongly about his or her own political views that he or she will attempt to belittle or berate anyone with a different belief or opinion. In those instances, a lady can either attempt to change the subject or do her best to end the conversation in a civil manner. A lady knows it is easier to change the subject than it is to change another person's mind.

## When a Lady Must Ask the Lady in the Next Stall in a Public Restroom for Some Toilet Paper . . .

*She does not say:*

"Have you got any toilet paper over there? Guess I forgot to look before it was too late."

"I'm not trying to freak you out, but if I stick my hand under the stall, would you hand me some toilet paper? This one is out."

*But she does say:*

"Excuse me, but there is no toilet tissue in this stall. May I ask you to pass me some, please?"

At times, a lady may find herself in an awkward situation that requires asking a complete stranger for assistance. In such instances, she is straightforward in asking for help. No matter how unconventional or inconvenient the situation, she always remembers her manners and expresses her simple gratitude for the assistance.

## WHEN A LADY HEARS A NEGATIVE COMMENT ABOUT HER RELIGION OR HER RELIGIOUS HERITAGE . . .

*She does not say:*

"I have been fighting bigots like you all of my life."

"You have got one of the best sixteenth-century minds I've ever encountered."

"We'll see who's laughing when you are burning in hell."

*But she does say:*

"I am deeply committed to my beliefs, just as I'm sure you are committed to yours. I respect that, and I hope you will respect me in the same way."

Or:

"I'm very proud of my heritage; just as I'm sure you are proud of your own. I would never make disparaging remarks about your heritage; I hope you'll show me the same respect."

A lady does not engage in disputes with ill-mannered, insensitive persons. Neither, however, does she shy away from making it clear that she finds ethnic and religious slurs inappropriate, in any situation.

# A LADY SAYS NO

A lady is not being unkind or insensitive when she uses the word *no*. She may indeed find it one of the most useful words in her vocabulary.

A lady has no responsibility to spend time with a man she finds boorish. She need not pressure herself to chair the school bake sale, when her schedule is already overcrowded. And she need not offer any explanation when asked to contribute to a political candidate with whom she does not agree. She knows she is doing no one a favor by agreeing to participate in a project for which she has no passion—or any free time. She knows, too, that she is wasting her money and her leisure time by agreeing to go on a singles cruise, on which she knows she will have a horrible time.

Because the request or invitation may be well intended, however, a lady is careful to offer her turndown in the kindest, least offensive way possible. She does not say, "No way, José" or "What could you possibly be thinking?" Instead, she simply says, "No. But thank you for asking."

If she still feels pressured by the request or invitation—particularly if it is an invitation for a date—a lady reemphasizes her response, saying, "I'm sorry, but no is my final answer. I'm sticking with that." In such situations, the lady may find it necessary to end the discussion by whatever method is convenient—whether that is walking away from the conversation or ending the telephone call.

Should a lady discover that her no is not being taken seriously in response to sexual advances, she takes whatever action is necessary to protect herself—fleeing the situation, alerting the restaurant manager, or calling the police department.

# GIVING, LENDING, BORROWING, AND SHARING

## WHEN A LADY IS APPROACHED BY A PANHANDLER, AND THE LADY CHOOSES NOT TO GIVE HIM OR HER MONEY . . .

*She does not say:*

"Why don't you get a job?"

"Sorry. All I've got is a hundred-dollar bill."

"Do you think I'm crazy? I know you're just a drunk."

"I'm sorry, I don't give money to people on the street—but I want you to know that I give big bucks to help people like you, and I also serve Thanksgiving lunch to the homeless."

*But she does say:*

Nothing, unless she knows the address of a nearby homeless shelter.

A lady decides for herself whether she wishes to give money—even in small amounts—to panhandlers. If a lady chooses to give to a panhandler, she does so discreetly, simply saying, "You're welcome," when she is thanked for her generosity. In no case does she risk her safety by preaching to a stranger of whose motivations she is uncertain.

WHEN AN ACQUAINTANCE ASKS A
LADY HOW MUCH SHE HAS PAID FOR
AN ITEM OF CLOTHING OR SOME
OTHER PERSONAL PROPERTY . . .

*She does not say:*

"Why are you asking?"

"I can't believe you'd ask that."

"Probably more than you could afford."

*But she does say:*

"Gee, I'm not sure I remember."

Whether this response is accurate or simply a means of escaping an awkward situation, it may short-circuit any further probing. If the nosy acquaintance continues to push, saying, "Oh, come now, that dress must have cost $750," a lady may simply close the discussion by saying, "I'm sorry, but I'd rather not talk about that."

## WHEN A LADY RECEIVES AN UNEXPECTED HOLIDAY GIFT FROM A FRIEND FOR WHOM SHE HAS NOT BOUGHT A PRESENT . . .

*She does not say:*
> "What are you doing giving me a present? I didn't get you anything."

> "I already got your present. I just haven't had time to get it wrapped."

> "Golly, I feel like dirt."

*But she does say:*
> "Thanks. Aren't you kind to think of me?"

True gifts are presented as tributes, not in hopes of recompense. If a lady receives an unexpected gift, she accepts it in the kindest way she can manage. She need not attempt to come up with a gift in return, after the fact. Instead, she makes sure to write an especially gracious thank-you note. If she wishes, she may make a point of remembering her generous friend when the next holiday season rolls around, but in truth she need only be grateful and make good use of her friend's gift.

WHEN A FRIEND ASKS TO BORROW A
LADY'S FAVORITE SWEATER OR SILVER TRAY
AND THE LADY WOULD PREFER NOT TO
LEND IT FOR FEAR IT WILL NOT BE
RETURNED . . .

*She does not say:*

"Sorry, but I'm sort of picky about the people I
lend my things to."

"Don't you know what that thing cost?"

"I'm sorry, but that belonged to my grandmother
and I would just die if you broke it."

"Are you sure you'll bring it back?"

*But she does say:*

"I wish I could help you, Monica, but I just don't
lend my silver. It's one of my private rules."

A lady does not openly question a friend's
integrity. If she prefers not to run the risk of
never having her silver punch bowl or sweater
returned, she simply does not lend it. When she
says this is her rule, whether it relates to lending
money or lending personal property, she sticks
to it, not favoring one friend over another.

WHEN A LADY, AT THE HEALTH CLUB,
WISHES TO USE A WORKOUT MACHINE
THAT ANOTHER MEMBER HAS BEEN
MONOPOLIZING . . .

*She does not say:*

"Are you gonna hog that machine all day?"

"Why don't you free up that machine for
somebody who *really* knows how to use it?"

"I'm in a real hurry. Just how many reps are you
gonna do?"

*But she does say:*

"While you're resting between sets, how about if I
cut in? Then, maybe we can switch off."

In any gym or health club, there are times
when there is not enough equipment to go
around. Unfortunately, those are the times
when boorish club members often choose to
work out. The best a lady can do is to offer to
share the equipment, perhaps by offering to
"spot" him or her on the next set of repetitions.
If the loutish club member's behavior continues,
a lady may wish to report him or her to the
management. She does not force the issue in
the middle of the workout room.

## When a lady is asked what she wants as a gift . . .

*She does not say:*

"Diamonds are a girl's best friend."

"A gift certificate or money, so that I can pick something that I *really* want."

"If it's not out of your price range, I would really like to have a place setting of my silver."

*But she does say:*

"You're kind to ask. But you have great taste. I'll leave it to your discretion."

A lady hopes that a friend or loved one will make the choice of a gift, based on good intentions and on their understanding of the lady's own tastes and preferences. If the question is inspired by the forthcoming birth of a baby or an upcoming wedding, a lady may simply explain that she is registered at a certain store or at various stores. Whatever the gift turns out to be, however, a lady says she appreciates it—and she means what she says.

# IN TIMES OF SADNESS

## When a lady's coworker has returned to work after the death of a loved one . . .

*She does not say:*

"Gee, I guess your work really stacked up while you were away."

"I wish my aunt would die so that I could take a day off."

"Were you close?"

"Were you in the will?"

*But she does say:*

"I'm sorry to hear about your uncle. Please let me know if there's anything I can do to help you get back into the swing of things here at work."

A lady may spend most of her waking hours with her coworkers, but she does not attempt to intrude into their private lives. Neither does she attempt to equate her family experience with theirs. Her task as a well-mannered fellow employee is to assist her friend in achieving the easiest possible reentry to the workplace. In doing so, she provides great comfort.

WHEN A LADY GREETS THE MOURNERS IN
THE RECEIVING LINE AT A VISITATION, A
WAKE, OR A FUNERAL . . .

*She does not say:*
"I guess you must actually be relieved."

"Charlie really hung on, didn't he?"

"Maybe your life can get back to normal now."

"Well, as they say, only the good die young."

*But she does say:*
"I'm so sorry about your loss. I've been thinking
about you a lot."

In times of grief, a lady is wise to keep her
comments simple, honest, and heartfelt. When
a friend has lost a child or a beloved parent,
words, no matter how eloquent, cannot possibly
fill the void. The friend might be confused by
futile attempts to find sunshine behind the
clouds, but she will retain memories of the
lady's warm embrace and gentle condolences.

# WHEN A LADY'S FRIEND HAS LOST A BABY . . .

*She does not say:*

"You're still young. Aren't you glad you can have more children?"

"It was meant to be."

"This was God's way of saying you weren't ready."

"It was probably for the best. Kids are so much work."

"Well, at least you already have one child."

*But she does say:*

"I've been thinking about you," or if she is a praying person, "I want you to know you've been in my prayers."

It is pointless, and even cruel, to attempt to rationalize such a tragedy. In such situations, a lady edits her words meticulously. Even if she has experienced a similar sadness, she does not urge her friend to relive his or her anguish. A close friend will let the lady know when he or she is ready to talk about this devastating experience. Until then, a lady expresses her sympathy in the simplest and most sincere manner possible.

## WHEN A FRIEND'S PET HAS DIED . . .

*She does not say:*

   "Did you have to put him to sleep?"

   "Well, he was pretty old for a dog."

   "Aren't you glad you can get a new puppy?"

   "I can't believe how upset you are. After all, it was just a cat."

*But she does say:*

   "I'm sorry about Fluffy. I know she meant a lot to you."

Whatever her opinion of pets and pet owners, a lady knows that many people love their animals as much as (and sometimes more than) their human families. A lady does not make light of the loss of a beloved animal; neither does she suggest that an adored companion can be easily replaced. For some pet owners, such a remark is as heartless as suggesting that a new husband or a wife can take the place of a lost partner.

## WHEN A LOVED ONE OF A LADY'S FRIEND OR COWORKER HAS COMMITTED SUICIDE . . .

*She does not say:*

"But he always seemed so *happy.*"

"That is so selfish."

"Now, I certainly hope you don't think this is your fault."

"You didn't find the body, did you?"

"Did she leave a note?"

*But she does say:*

"I'm so sorry to hear about Paula. Please know I've been thinking about you."

This is exactly the same comment a lady makes whenever a friend has lost a loved one, whatever the cause. The added trauma of suicide need not be noted. Neither is it the lady's task to raise troubling questions that her friend is very likely already facing.

## WHEN A LADY LEARNS THAT THE DECEASED LOVED ONE OF A FRIEND OR COWORKER HAS BEEN CREMATED . . .

*She does not say:*

"I couldn't do that."

"What did his parents say?"

"I'm not sure that's right. My religion doesn't allow it."

"Don't you feel sorta weird, having Sam's ashes right there in the house?"

*But she does say:*

"I wish I could have made it to the funeral. I understand it was a lovely service."

A lady's personal opinion about cremation is of no importance—unless she is having to decide upon a loved one's form of burial or is planning her own funeral. Some religious traditions do not permit cremation, but it is increasingly accepted as an option in many mainline faiths. The choice of cremation says nothing about the esteem in which the dearly departed was held.

## WHEN THE LOVED ONE OF A LADY'S FRIEND OR COWORKER HAS BEEN KILLED IN AN AUTOMOBILE ACCIDENT . . .

*She does not say:*
"I bet she wasn't wearing her seat belt, was she?"

"Do they think the wreck was his fault?"

"How fast was he going?"

"Was there alcohol involved?"

"I certainly hope the other guy had insurance."

*But she does say:*
"This is a horrible blow, Mary. Please know that you are in my thoughts."

Unless she is working as an officer of the law, a lady does not ask probing questions at such a sensitive time. Neither does she make assumptions about guilt or innocence. She simply expresses her concern in the most direct way possible.

## When a lady greets the boyfriend or girlfriend of the deceased at a memorial service . . .

*She does not say:*

"Don't you wish now that you'd gotten married?"

"Guess you're glad now you didn't tie the knot."

"You're young. You'll find somebody else right away."

"Are you going to sit with the family at the service?"

"Do you know if you were in the will?"

*But she does say:*

"I'm sorry, Jill (or Jerry). You and Jerry (or Jill) were such a wonderful couple."

A lady never presumes that she knows all the details about the personal relationship of two other people. Especially in a time of grief, she does not probe for information; neither does she discuss what might have been. More important, she does not assume that, because no legal documents were signed, a boyfriend or girlfriend was not as cherished as a church-sanctioned spouse. The pain is just as real.

# AWKWARDNESS
# EXTRAORDINAIRE

WHEN A FRIEND SHOWS A LADY A PICTURE
OF HIS NEW CHILD OR GRANDCHILD, AND
THE BABY, AT LEAST IN THE LADY'S
OPINION, IS LESS THAN ADORABLE . . .

*She does not say:*
"What's wrong with his head?"

"I bet his mother's crazy about him anyhow,
isn't she?"

"Don't worry. They grow out of that stage really
quickly."

"Well, that sure is a baby."

*But she does say:*
"Gee, Leslie, I'll bet you're really proud."

Truth to tell, few babies look their best in
their neonatal photos. A lady will be wise to
proceed cautiously, even in the best of cases,
sticking to vapid exclamations of admiration
such as "Isn't she cute?" or "Look at those tiny
little fingers!" In such cases, as long as "she"
does not turn out to be a "he," a lady can never
go wrong.

## When a lady's close lady friend asks if she looks fat (and she does) . . .

*She does not say:*

"No, actually I thought you'd lost weight."

"Who am I to ask? Look how much weight I've gained."

"Maybe it's just those slacks."

"Why worry? Some guys like their women sort of chunky."

*But she does say:*

"You're a great-looking woman (or a beautiful one, if she means it). If you've gained a little weight, you've got the style to carry it off."

A lady attempts to avoid lying, at any cost. When a lady friend asks this question, in most cases she already knows the answer. She's the one who checks the scales every morning; she's the one who just struggled to fit into the size eight jeans that fit perfectly a couple of weeks ago. The kindest, and most honest, course is to offer reinforcement and reassurance. A lady knows that sort of response will never come back to haunt her.

## WHEN A LADY'S UNMARRIED WOMAN FRIEND TELLS HER SHE IS PREGNANT AND PLANS TO KEEP THE BABY . . .

*She does not say:*

"Well, gee, Gloria, don't you think a child should have two parents?"

"Do you know who the father is?"

"What's the matter? Couldn't you get him to marry you?"

*But she does say:*

"Congratulations. You'll make a wonderful mother."

If her friend is sharing the news of her pregnancy, a lady may assume that she is not ashamed of her condition. She greets the news with the same good wishes she would offer any expectant mother. The mother-to-be is probably well aware of the challenges before her; she does not need the lady's reminders, no matter how well intentioned.

## WHEN A LADY MUST BREAK
## A SOCIAL COMMITMENT . . .

*She does not say:*

"I'm sorry, Anne, but I won't be able to make your party. Something more important has come up."

"Sorry, Chuck, we've got to reschedule dinner. Robby just called with tickets to *Hairspray.*"

*But she does say:*

"I'm sorry, Ann, but we can't make it tonight. I just received a deadline for Monday, and it means no playtime this weekend. I hope you'll let me have a raincheck."

There are times when a lady must change—or cancel—her plans. In no case, however, does she cancel a social obligation simply because something more appealing has come up. When she calls to express her regrets, she clearly states her *actual* reason for bowing out, such as an unexpected work deadline, a death in the family, or an unexpected illness. She apologizes straightforwardly and, if appropriate, attempts to reschedule the outing.

## When it is necessary for a lady to make an apology . . .

*She does not say:*

"I understand you think I owe you an apology."

"Sorry if I hurt your feelings."

"Sometimes people just don't know when I'm joking."

*But she does say:*

"Millie, I'm sorry if I offended you the other evening when I commented on your leather pants. I'd had too many glasses of wine and said something I shouldn't have."

A lady makes it clear that she understands an apology is in order—even if she truly meant no offense. She does not act as if she is being coerced into apologizing; neither does she attempt to downplay any embarrassment or discomfort she might have caused. Once she has apologized, she does not raise the subject again. To do so is to reopen a gradually healing wound.

## WHEN A LADY IS OFFERED AN APOLOGY . . .

*She does not say:*

"I guess you expect me to believe you really mean that."

"I know you're not sorry; you're just sorry I heard you."

"All right, but don't let it happen again."

"'I'm sorry' isn't good enough."

*But she does say:*

"I accept your apology, Eva. I was hurt, I admit, and I appreciate your concern for my feelings. Now let's just move on."

Unless a lady has been offended repeatedly by the same person, she accepts an apology at face value. She does not pretend that the offense never happened, but she makes it clear that she has now put the awkwardness behind her. She might not fully forgive, or fully forget, but she does not dwell on past unpleasantness.

## WHEN A FRIEND TELLS A LADY THAT HE IS GAY OR SHE IS A LESBIAN . . .

*She does not say to him:*

"Duh. I knew that the first time I met you. I was waiting for you to figure it out."

"Thank God—I had the biggest crush on you and was devastated when you were not interested."

"Funny, you don't act gay."

*She does not say to her:*

"Well, that's fine. Just don't get any ideas about me."

"But you're so feminine."

"What a shame."

*But she does say:*

"I'm glad you feel comfortable telling me, Carson (or Carla)."

A lady realizes that despite the tolerance of the day, even a good friend might hesitate before revealing that he or she is gay. Even if she does not approve of her friend's sexual orientation, a lady is glad that her friend has taken her into his or her confidence. She does not pry into the details of the sex lives of her friends, be they homosexual or heterosexual.

WHEN A FRIEND TELLS A LADY THAT HIS OR
HER CHILD (OR SIBLING) IS GAY, AND THE
LADY IS NOT SURE WHETHER THE FAMILY IS
HAPPY ABOUT THE REVELATION . . .

*She does not say:*

"Maybe it's just a phase."

"I'm so sorry. I know you always wanted
grandchildren."

"I always knew—but I didn't have the heart to
tell you."

"Well, at least you'll never have to hire a decorator."

*But she does say:*

"Dave (or Delia) is such a wonderful person.
That's the thing that really matters."

Unless the friend presses her for further
discussion of the matter, a lady does not offer her
opinions or advice. If the friend seems truly
distressed by the news, a lady may suggest that
the friend talk to a minister or counselor. If the
friend seems to be taking the news with little
distress, a lady may say, "I hope things continue to
go well." In no case does she attempt to bring her
personal moral conventions into the conversation.

## WHEN THE LOVED ONE OF A LADY'S FRIEND OR COWORKER IS HAVING LEGAL TROUBLE, OR IS EVEN IN PRISON . . .

*She does not say:*

"Are you going to go visit him?"

"Hold you head up. You're not the one who's guilty."

"What's it like in prison? Is it like it looks in the movies?"

"This is the time when you will find out who your true friends are."

*But she does say:*

"Have you had a chance to talk to Tobias? How's he getting along?"

A lady does not ignore the fact that a friend is going through difficult times. However, she does not sensationalize the situation, probing for details that she can then recycle through the rumor mill. She may wish to add a comment such as, "I can only imagine how tough this is. Let me know what I can do to help." She might even offer to assist a coworker (from time to time, not on an ongoing basis) in keeping up with his or her workload.

## WHEN A LADY'S FRIEND ANNOUNCES THAT HER PARENTS HAVE BEEN MOVED TO A NURSING HOME . . .

*She does not say:*

"Is it a good one?"

"I'll bet that made you feel guilty, didn't it?"

"Well, I'd certainly never do that to my parents."

"I hope my kids never do that to me."

"Didn't I see a story about that place on the news the other night?"

*But she does say:*

"How are your parents doing, Evan? Are they settling in all right?"

A lady might have no idea of all the factors that have led her friend to make this decision. Neither does she assume that the friend's parents are opposed to the move. She expresses her concern but otherwise keeps her opinions to herself. And she never adds to her friend's worries by sharing horror stories gleaned from the nightly news. If the friend cares about such stories, she is probably keeping up with them herself.

# WHEN A LADY FEELS SHE HAS BEEN PAID A BACKHANDED COMPLIMENT . . .

*She does not say:*
   "Thank you . . . I think?"

   "You need to work on your manners."

   "What do you mean, 'For a big girl I have a
   pretty face'?"

   "I guess you meant that as a compliment."

*But she does say:*
   "Thank you."

A lady tries to think the best of everyone. She realizes that not everyone is a silver-tongued orator, and she assumes that, no matter how awkwardly phrased, a compliment is always offered with the kindest of intentions. In the same way that she would never correct another person's grammar in public, she does not question the motivation behind a quirky compliment. She accepts it for its good intentions and then moves on with her life.

## When a lady declines a social invitation . . .

*She does not say:*

"Sorry, Kim, I wouldn't be comfortable at your party. Your crowd makes me feel weird."

"Gee, wish I could make it, but my favorite show is on TV that night."

"I'll have to see. I've got a lot of reading to do."

*But she does say:*

"I'm sorry, Zoe, but I won't be able to make it. I've already got a commitment."

As a rule, a lady does not decline a social invitation unless she has a prior commitment. (Even if she is not fond of her would-be host's friends, she can at least stop by for a few minutes to demonstrate her gratitude for being invited.) If there are serious reasons for her declining the invitation—she will be uncomfortable with the guests' behavior or with the presence of alcohol or drugs—she declines graciously but firmly, without further elaboration. But a lady knows that a television show is never a good excuse for refusing a friend's hospitality.

## WHEN AN ACQUAINTANCE ASKS A LADY
## IF HER JEWELRY IS REAL . . .

*She does not say:*

"Do I look like one of those tacky women who would wear a cubic zirconium?"

"Yes, it's real, and it cost more than $15,000."

"It's a fake. Do you think I'd wear my real jewelry in this neighborhood?"

"I'll tell you, if you tell me if that's your real nose."

*But she does say:*

"Yes" or "No," or nothing at all.

It is a lady's prerogative to decide how she wishes to handle such questions. She may wish to respond with an interesting detail, such as "Yes, it belonged to my Aunt Tess, and I really treasure it" or "No, I picked this up at a yard sale for a dollar; can you believe it?" On the other hand, a lady always has the option of ignoring an intrusive question by simply saying, "I'm glad you like it" and then proceeding to change the subject.

## When a Lady is Introduced to a Person with an Unusual Last Name . . .

*She does not say:*

"You must have had a terrible time in school with that name."

"Has anyone ever spelled your name correctly?"

"You mean your married name is Lola Honeybone? I don't care how great he is. I couldn't have married him."

"Have you ever thought about changing that name?"

*But she does say:*

"It's a pleasure to meet you."

Only in the rarest of circumstances does a person have anything do with the choice of his or her last name. At some point in the conversation, a lady may wish to say, "Excuse me, I would like to remember your last name. Would you mind repeating it for me?" But under no conditions does a lady laugh, make wisecracks, or risk making a new acquaintance feel uncomfortable or self-conscious.

## WHEN A LADY FEELS HER FRIENDS HAVE CHOSEN AN UNFORTUNATE NAME FOR THEIR NEW BABY . . .

*She does not say:*

"Who came up with that name? The poor child will be scarred for life."

"Is that name supposed to be a joke?"

"No amount of inheritance is going to make up for living with a name like 'Lucifer.'"

*But she does say:*

"And what a cute, cute baby he is . . ."

A lady knows that naming rights belong to a baby's family. In no case does she comment negatively about a child's name, since it may be the name of a beloved relative or may hold some special significance for the parents.

## WHEN AN ACQUAINTANCE COMMENTS
## ON A LADY'S THINNESS . . .

*She does not say:*

"Let me tell you about my new fruit-only diet . . ."

"I would just die if I were fat."

"I'm not sick, and I don't have an eating
disorder—if that's what you were thinking."

*But she does say:*

"Thank you; it's the result of healthy living."

A lady's body image is a very personal
thing. And if she is happy with her appearance
and her health is good, she dismisses probing
questions. However, if she hears from numerous
people, especially from those who love her, that
she is too thin, she takes stock of her eating
habits and her exercise program—and she
consults a physician.

## When a friend or acquaintance asks a single lady why she has never married . . .

*She does not say:*

"All the good ones are gay or married."

"I don't need a man to make my life complete."

"I am dying to get married. Do you know anyone?"

*But she does say:*

"That just hasn't been on my agenda."

A lady of a certain age may have her own reasons for remaining unmarried. Whatever those reasons, they are nobody's business but her own, and she need not share them with anyone except her closest friends. Especially at pleasant social occasions, and in business situations, she does not seize the moment to make herself sound like a victim or to share her history with unfaithful love interests. Neither does she go into a detailed defense of her decision to remain an independent, unmarried woman.

## WHEN A VISITOR MAKES A DEROGATORY COMMENT ABOUT THE DÉCOR OF A LADY'S HOME . . .

*She does not say:*

"I feel the same way about that dress you're wearing."

"Well, you obviously have no taste, since we used a top interior designer."

"Well, between you and me, I hate it too—but Reggie's mom gave us that rolltop desk, and she'd cut us out of the will if we didn't put it here in the living room."

*But she does say:*

"I appreciate your opinion. But it feels just like home to us."

It is perfectly acceptable for a lady to respond forthrightly to a rude comment. She need not defend herself for decorating her home in a manner she can afford, much less in a way that she finds attractive—and one that suits her lifestyle.

## When a lady overhears a racial, ethnic, sexist, or homophobic slur . . .

*She does not say:*

"Is there *anybody* you won't insult?"

"Intolerance is so ugly, Phyllis. I thought you were better than that."

"Watch it. When you make jokes like that, you're talking about some of my best friends."

*But she does say:*

"There is no excuse for remarks of that nature, and I find them objectionable. Let's please change the subject."

A lady does not allow friends, social acquaintances, or coworkers to infer that she has any tolerance for bigoted comments or tasteless jokes. She does not engage the ill-mannered boor in an argument, but she does stand by her convictions, making it clear that she finds such language or comments inappropriate. Without appearing high-handed or haughty, she simply walks away from the situation, confident that she will find better-mannered company and more tasteful conversation some other place and at some other time.

## WHEN A LADY'S FRIEND OR ACQUAINTANCE RAMBLES ON ABOUT HER CHILDREN OR GRANDCHILDREN . . .

*She does not say:*

"When you finish telling me about yours, I'll tell you about mine—if there's still any time left."

"You've changed so much since you had that baby. You're not the same person."

"I'm glad I'm not one of those women who stopped being her own person when she had a baby."

*But she does say:*

"I'm glad your kids are doing so well. Have you heard anything from Marjorie lately?"

Parents, especially new parents and new grandparents, love to talk about their children. At the same time, unfortunately, they are often prone to forget that other people may have a limited interest in hearing about little Liam's potty training. A lady does her best to listen politely, since she understands that the topic of Liam's potty training is of tremendous importance to her friend, but she knows how to change the subject of any conversation gracefully and graciously.

## WHEN A MAN INAPPROPRIATELY REFERS TO A LADY AS "HONEY" OR "BABE" . . .

*She does not say:*

"This is the twenty-first century. I didn't know there were any Neanderthals like you still running around out there."

"Is this how you address every woman you work with, or is it just me?"

"You'll think 'Honey,' when I slap you with a harassment lawsuit."

*But she does say:*

"My name is Sheryl, not 'Honey.'"

A lady may find it endearing for some gentlemen—such as her husband, her love interest, or her father—to use pet names. But her coworkers, her casual acquaintances, and male employees in the service industries do not fall into that category. If a male coworker uses unprofessional language, she makes it clear that his behavior is inappropriate. If his behavior continues, she takes her complaint to his supervisor. In no case does she attempt to shrug off the insult, as if it were simply a burden to be accepted as part of life.

## When a lady is traveling alone and needs assistance . . .

*She does not say:*

"I'm not trying to get fresh, but could you help me with my luggage?"

"Ever since the Women's Movement, I guess all you big guys are afraid to help a little lady."

"Are you just going to stand there while I hurt myself, or are you going to be a gentleman?"

*But she does say:*

"Would you be kind enough to help me put my bag in the overhead compartment?"

Although a lady may be an experienced solo traveler, like any other traveler, she may sometimes require assistance with luggage, directions, or a foreign language. A lady knows that she is not belittling herself when she asks for assistance that is truly needed. She knows, in fact, that asking for assistance, early on, may forestall a potentially troublesome, or even dangerous, situation. When she asks for assistance, she does so in a direct, unapologetic manner, graciously thanking anyone who has lent a helping hand.

# WHEN GOOD GIRLS GO BAD

*Talking Your Way Out of Trouble*
*When You've Blown It, Big Time*

She may monitor her speech meticulously. She may say please and thank you. She may refuse to talk about politics at the dinner table. But once in a while, every lady, even the most scrupulous one, is going to put her foot in her mouth or commit a *faux pas* so ghastly that a simple apology may not be enough. A lady never intentionally offends another person, but she sometimes makes a mistake of seemingly colossal proportions. The following are instances of the sort that might doom even the most well-meaning lady to a lifelong diet of humble pie—along with advice as to how she might possibly salvage the situation.

WHEN A LADY REALIZES SHE HAS SPENT TOO MUCH TIME TELLING HER DATE HOW HANDSOME SHE THINKS ANOTHER MAN IS . . .

As quickly as possible, she changes the subject. What's more, if she is wise, she shifts the subject to one that actually interests her companion. She may choose to ask him about an important project at his office, or she may ask his opinion about a column in the newspaper. If her date persists in pursuing the subject, a lady states simply, "Yes. He is a good-looking fellow, and he was certainly using all his charms this evening." At no point during the remainder of the evening does she say, "You know, that's precisely what Fred was saying."

WHEN A LADY REALIZES TWO DAYS AFTER A HEATED ARGUMENT THAT SHE WAS IN THE WRONG . . .

She shows her true mettle by admitting her mistake. Such an admission is, in fact, about the grandest possible demonstration of ladylike behavior. She need only say, "Roxanne, I've realized that you were right the other day when we were talking about how many times Elizabeth Taylor has been married. I was wrong. I should be more careful to get my facts right."

WHEN A LADY HAS LOST HER TEMPER AND RAISED HER VOICE TO HER ADMINISTRATIVE ASSISTANT, OR TO ANY OTHER COWORKER . . .

In such cases, a lady can only pray that she has not made any idle threats or given any ultimatums. If she is lucky, she will get by with a simple, honest apology, saying, "Forgive me for yelling at you, Charlie. It was entirely out of line. There was no excuse for my behavior." If she has, however, made statements she must retract, she does so as soon as possible, before they circulate around the office. She sets the record straight as clearly as possible, saying, "I didn't mean what I said about your salary the other day, Charlie. I'm sorry. Please know that I value your work."

If a lady discovers that she is given to rages or outbursts of temper, she will be well advised to consult a physician or a counselor.

WHEN A LADY HAS MADE HERSELF, AND HER DATE, LATE FOR AN IMPORTANT EVENT, SIMPLY BECAUSE SHE WASN'T READY ON TIME . . .

A lady does not make light of such thoughtless behavior. She does not attempt to dismiss the situation by saying, "Well, everybody's always late at these affairs, anyhow," or "I hear the first half of the show isn't all that interesting, anyway." Instead, because a lady does not offer empty apologies, she accepts full responsibility for her tardiness,

promises to amend her behavior in the future—
and then does so. She does not, however, ruin
the entire evening by continuing to bring up
the subject of her lateness, as though she were
begging for forgiveness and reassurance.

If a lady realizes, far enough ahead of time,
that she will be running considerably late, she
may even give her date a call, suggesting that
they arrive separately at the event. Such an
arrangement may seem awkward and even
embarrassing—but it is no more awkward than
asking her date to miss the kick-off for the big
game, or the salad course at a dinner party.

WHEN A LADY REALIZES THAT SHE HAS, IN
TRUTH, SAID SOMETHING THAT HAS HURT
ANOTHER PERSON'S FEELINGS . . .

A lady makes a straightforward apology,
avoiding all temptation to make excuses for
herself. The best apology is the simplest: "Jeri,
I'm afraid I hurt your feelings the other night.
Please know I'm sorry. I didn't mean to offend
you." It is never a lady's place to decide whether
another person has any right to be offended.
Even if she is convinced she was not in the
wrong, at least she has done her best to stay on

cordial terms with a person whose opinion she values. If the offended person continues to take umbrage, prolonging the pain by saying, "That was one of the ugliest things anybody's ever said to me. I've been telling everybody about it," the lady can only repeat her initial apology: "Again, let me say I'm sorry to have hurt your feelings." After that, she tries to change the subject, leaves the room, or considers whether she is perhaps wasting too much energy on this particular friendship.

## WHEN A LADY MUST FACE A MAN WHO HAS MADE HER CRY IN A BUSINESS SITUATION . . .

A lady handles such situations as privately as possible, asking her business colleague for a face-to-face meeting, in a setting that is beyond their coworkers' earshot. (She does not suggest that they "have a drink and talk it over.") If her business colleague has brought her to tears through his own boorish behavior, a lady offers no apology for her behavior. Instead, she tells him, forthrightly, "Jim, our encounter this morning got entirely out of hand. Even if you don't respect my opinion, I expect you to watch your language in the future." If the lady realizes that her emotions have got the best of her—just as a gentleman's anger sometimes gets the best of him—she apologizes simply and directly, saying, "Jim, my behavior this morning was inappropriate. I hope you'll forgive me for creating an awkward situation."

Better yet, however, when a lady realizes that her emotions may be getting out of hand, she excuses herself from the situation—just as a gentleman would do, should his temper get the best of him.